A Literary Tour *of* DEVON

by
Paul Wreyford

'This book is dedicated to Denise and Paul'

First published in Great Britain in 1996

Copyright © Paul Wreyford

ORCHARD PUBLICATIONS
2 Orchard Close, Chudleigh, Newton Abbot, Devon TQ13 0LR
Telephone: (01626) 852714

All rights reserved. No part of this publication may be reproduced, stored in a retrieval system, or transmitted in any form or by any means, without the prior permission of the copyright holder.

ISBN 1 898964 21 1

Designed, Typeset and Printed for Orchard Publications by
Swift Print
2 High Street
Dawlish
Devon EX7 9HP

PREFACE

It is no coincidence Devon has so many literary connections. There are few better places where an aspiring or established scribe could gain inspiration. The county is home to almost every habitat imaginable - from lush green valleys and secluded coves, to desolate moorland and dramatic rocky headlands. Native writers have been inspired by the natural landscape while others have flocked to it to seek that inspiration.

Most areas in Devon have some connection with famous literary figures and some parts have earned immortal fame thanks to the pen of novelists and poets.

Creepy Dartmoor is home to Arthur Conan Doyle's, The Hound of the Baskervilles, while the beautiful scenery of Exmoor on the North Devon and Somerset coast has R.D. Blackmore's Lorna Doone to thank for its share of visitors.

The south coast of Devon - with its popular holiday destinations - could not be more inviting, but this is where native crime writer Agatha Christie set many of her murders!

Much of North Devon has been re-christened Tarka Country after Henry Williamson's classic, Tarka the Otter.

There is hardly a place in Devon which has not been blessed with some literary association.

Home-grown talent includes Samuel Taylor Coleridge (East Devon); Charles Kingsley and John Gay (North Devon).

Those who made their home in the county include John Galsworthy (Dartmoor); J.A. Froude and Robert Graves (South Devon).

The visiting list is endless: Jane Austen, Charles Dickens, Lord Alfred Tennyson, Geoffrey Chaucer, Thomas Hardy, John Keats, Beatrix Potter, Anthony Trollope, Oscar Wilde and, of course, the famous Romantic poets, to name but a few!

Novelists, short-story writers, poets, historians and hymn-writers have all been inspired by the beauty of Devon. Many are featured over the next few pages.

CONTENTS

Page No.

INTRODUCTION   3

Chapter One: EXMOOR   4
    Principal author - R.D. Blackmore

Chapter Two: TARKA COUNTRY   11
    Principal author - Henry Williamson

Chapter Three: NORTH DEVON   17
    Principal author - Charles Kingsley

Chapter Four: DARTMOOR   24
    Principal author - Arthur Conan Doyle

Chapter Five: PLYMOUTH AND SOUTH DEVON   36
    Principal author - Thomas Hardy

Chapter Six: TORBAY   46
    Principal author - Agatha Christie

Chapter Seven: EXETER   57
    Principal author - Charles Dickens

Chapter Eight: EAST DEVON   68
    Principal author - Samuel Taylor Coleridge

INTRODUCTION

Treading in the footsteps of the famous has always been a fascinating pastime. In the case of writers it is even more enthralling. To explore the places which fired their imagination and inspired them to pen some of our favourite novels and poems is an enlightening experience.

This book aims to take the reader to those places and to reveal the stories behind the stories! The reader is taken around the county via eight grand literary tours. Within these tours are numerous smaller tours which can be tackled individually. This means the visitor can pick a tour of their favourite author or select an area they are particularly interested in.

Tours vary in length, giving something for the long-distance walker or motorist, as well as those just out for an afternoon stroll. Individual literary locations can also be picked out for those wishing to do barely any walking at all!

Fortunately, large areas of Devon have remained unchanged from the days when many of the country's great writers were influenced by it. In the majority of cases, the reader should have little difficulty matching fiction to real-life.

Many of the original buildings occupied by our literary greats still stand. The reader will be taken to these and any other places of interest connected with the author. Of course, the bulldozer has occasionally reared its ugly head over the years, so in some cases, a little imagination may be required to gain the same inspiration first sought by the writer!

Maps indicating literary locations are included, though in some cases, an additional detailed Ordnance Survey map may be required. Some places were deliberately chosen by writers for their solitude and sign-posts may not be in abundance!

While this is a thorough guide - more than 100 writers are featured - it does not claim to be exhaustive. It would be impossible to list every literary connection in Devon. Many writers have come to the area and gone away unnoticed in their bid for solitude. I am also painfully aware there are too many writers to list in a book of this size. I can only apologise to fellow scribes - dead or alive - who may feel aggrieved at not being included!

Paul Wreyford

EXMOOR

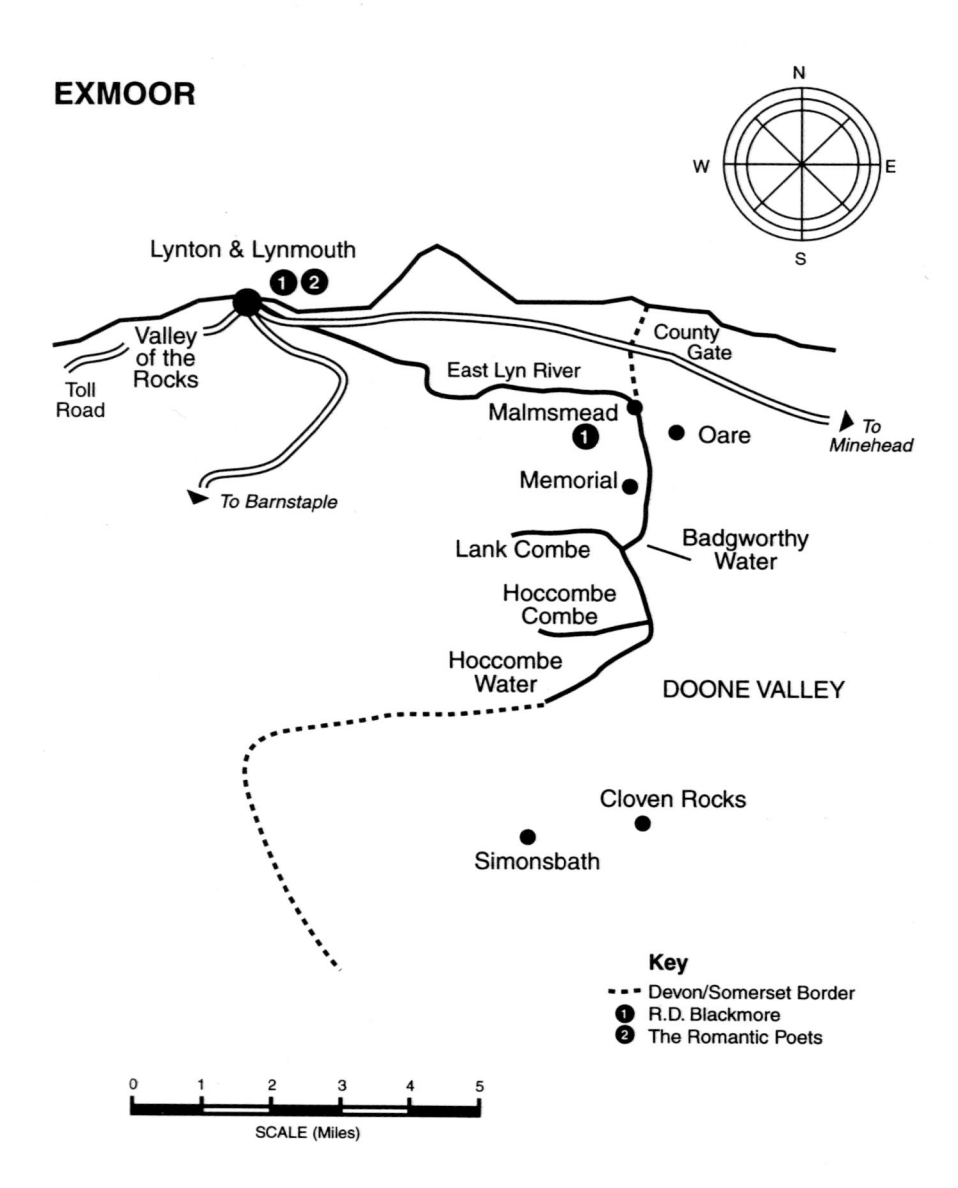

Part of beautiful Exmoor - the country's smallest national park - falls within the county of Devon. On the boundary with Somerset you will find Lorna Doone Country - named after R.D. Blackmore's classic historical romance. The area has become one of the most-popular literary locations in the country. Exmoor was also visited and made famous by the English Romantic poets - Shelley, Wordsworth, Coleridge and Southey.

The beautiful and often stunning scenery makes a visit here even more special.

R.D. BLACKMORE

Novelist Richard Doddridge Blackmore was born in Oxfordshire, but spent most of his childhood in North Devon.

Lorna Doone, published in 1869, became one of the classics of English Literature and brought tourists flocking to this rural part of the country.

Places to see: Lorna Doone Country: Malmsmead - Doone Valley.
Lynton and Lynmouth: Valley of the Rocks - Lee Abbey.
Charles: Charles Church.

It is difficult to believe peaceful Exmoor may have once been inhabited by a marauding family of outlaws. The notorious Doones were exiled from their native Scotland in the 17th century because of a clash over land. They are believed to have settled in a valley lying on the Devon/Somerset border. The legend of the Doones - and their murderous and thieving ways - inspired one of the most-popular novels ever written. R.D. Blackmore's Lorna Doone brought remote Exmoor lasting fame. Few dared venture into Doone Valley in Blackmore's classic tale - though few dare leave the area without doing so these days! Visitors flock to the beautiful region to trace the steps of hero John Ridd, the man who dared confront the evil Doones.

Most people wishing to explore the area choose to use the delightful twin resorts of Lynton and Lynmouth as a base. Blackmore did likewise. He began the novel while he lodged at the Rising Sun Inn in Lynmouth in 1865. He would walk across the moor to collect information and view the places he wished to use in the book. The author could not have known where the Doones really lived as there was no Doone Valley on Exmoor - the name was given to the area because of the book and it has stuck ever since. Nowadays, the area around Lank Combe, on the west bank of Badgworthy Water, is accepted as Doone Valley, though there are doubts whether this was the home of the Doones or whether Blackmore even based their home there!

Not that this bothers the many tourists who come here and it should not deter you.

Doone Valley is about five miles from Lynton. It can be reached via a beautiful walk along the East Lyn River or by the A39 road. A perfect place to enter the valley is at picturesque Malmsmead. Here you will find Lorna Doone Farm next to a beautiful ford. It is a fine place to begin a walk along the stream into the heart of Lorna Doone Country. Badgworthy Water runs its course along the Devon/Somerset border. A path takes the walker along it into Doone Valley.

The first item of interest you will come across is a stone memorial erected in honour of Blackmore. It is situated on the bank of the river, opposite Cloud Farm. John Ridd's waterslide is reputed to be at Lank Combe, which meets Badgworthy Water from the west. This is where John entered Glen Doone and met Lorna for the first time.

At the southern end of the valley is Hoccombe Combe. The ruined houses are said to have once belonged to the Doone settlement. The complete walk from Malmsmead to Hoccombe Combe is less than three miles. An alternative route back to Malmsmead is available.

Many visitors like to journey over the border into Somerset and to Cloven Rocks - the reputed site of the Wizard's Slough. This is where John Ridd and Carver Doone confront each other for the final time, ending with the latter's demise in the 'black bog'. Cloven Rocks can be found just east of Simonsbath on the Challacombe to Exford road.

Oare Church - scene of the dramatic altar-shooting which prompted John to confront Carver - is also situated over the border and within easy reach of Malmsmead.

It is difficult to pinpoint many of the locations in the book and it is probable Blackmore used his imagination as opposed to fact for most of them. The visitor will need to do the same. There are, of course, some places which the visitor will have no problem recognising from the novel. One such place is the spectacular Valley of the Rocks on the outskirts of Lynton. The valley can be reached by road from Lynton or by the coastal footpath from Lynmouth. The dramatic steep hills, capped by huge granite rocks, are believed to have been formed more than 10,000 years ago. In the book, the valley is used as the home of the wise old hermit, Mother Melldrum. She shelters within the rock known as the Devil's Cheesewring and is believed to be based on a real person. John goes to her to talk about his love for Lorna and is warned to stay away from the Doones. He later witnesses a dramatic cliff-top fight in the valley between a sheep and a goat. Just around the corner from here is Lee

Abbey, once known as Ley Manor, the home of Baron De Whichehalse, who is in league with the Doones. The abbey is now a Christian conference centre, but well worth a visit for the fine views it affords.

Many more Devon places receive a mention in the book, such as North Molton, which is home to John's famous highwayman cousin Tom Faggus.

Blackmore came to the county at the age of six in 1831. His father accepted a curacy at Culmstock in the Blackdown Hills, east of Tiverton. A move to North Devon and Ashford, near Barnstaple, followed later. The Blackmore family had its roots in Exmoor. The youngster frequently stayed with his grandfather who was rector of Combe

The dramatic Valley of the Rocks was home to the hermit, Mother Melldrum, in R.D. Blackmore's Lorna Doone.

Martin and Oare, and his uncle who was rector of Charles, a little village on the fringes of the moor, six miles north-west of South Molton. A tablet commemorating Blackmore can be found in the church at the latter. The young Blackmore left to study at Oxford and spent the final 40 years of his life in London, though he still regarded Devon as his home. He is remembered solely for Lorna Doone, though he did write other novels, including Perlycross, which was based on Culmstock and Christowell, which was set on Dartmoor as opposed to Exmoor. It is difficult to believe Lorna Doone nearly faded into obscurity after being published. Of the first 500 copies printed - only 300 were sold!

THE ROMANTIC POETS

Percy Shelley, William Wordsworth, Samuel Taylor Coleridge and Robert Southey were known as the Romantic Poets.
They all knew Exmoor well and used its beautiful surroundings from which to draw inspiration.

Places to see: Lynton and Lynmouth: Shelley's Cottage - Valley of the Rocks.

The beautiful resorts of Lynton and Lynmouth sit alone on the north coast with only the expanse of the sea and wild Exmoor surrounding them. They form the only real base for people wishing to explore this beautiful part of the country and therefore attract numerous visitors. It is also hardly surprising the country's leading poets fell in love with the area.
Most visitors who first set eyes on Lynmouth will want to prolong their stay for as long as possible - they certainly will not want to leave as hastily as Percy Shelley! Not that the great poet left through choice. He came to the resort in the summer of 1812 with his 16-year-old bride Harriet Westbrook. They came largely to escape the wrath of the young girl's furious parents. The poet, only 19 himself, had also just discovered his father was refusing to support him financially. Shelley had recently been expelled from Oxford University for his atheist views and the hurried wedding was the last straw!
Shelley was not prepared to hold his tongue even in quiet Lynmouth, however. He regularly wrote political pamphlets and placed them in bottles to drop into the sea. Other pamphlets were launched in balloons from the top of a hill. The Government were alerted to his activities when his manservant was caught distributing seditious posters in Barnstaple. Officials raced to Lynmouth in order to keep a watch on Shelley, but by the time they arrived he had gone. Mr and Mrs Shelley had fled across to Wales in a rowing boat. Shelley did stay long enough to pen Queen Mab. The cottage at which the couple resided during their eventful nine weeks was sadly destroyed by fire in 1907, but was later rebuilt and renamed after the poet. Shelley's Cottage is now a hotel and restaurant.
Percy Shelley is one of the four poets remembered at the Modelgate Shelter in the Valley of the Rocks. The shelter, often called Poets' Corner, was erected to honour him and fellow scribes Wordsworth, Coleridge and Southey. It contains some of their most-famous poems.
The Romantic Poets loved this part of the country and would regularly enjoy walks in the area. The common link which brought them to the north coast of Devon was Devonian Samuel Taylor Coleridge. He lived for a spell across

Shelley's Cottage at Lynmouth.

The Modelgate Shelter honours the four Romantic Poets who regularly visited the Valley of the Rocks.

the Somerset border at Nether Stowey. He regularly took his literary friends along the coast to Lynton and Lynmouth. Robert Southey described Lynmouth as a Swiss village and the Valley of the Rocks as one of the wonders of the West Country. Southey and Coleridge were related by their marriages to two sisters.

The Wordsworths - William and Dorothy - also joined Coleridge on his many jaunts into Devon. The latter said they became 'three persons with one soul' when they were together. Coleridge and William Wordsworth were great friends and produced the Lyrical Ballads together. The Valley of the Rocks became the setting for The Wanderings of Cain. It was also going to be used for another joint Coleridge/Wordsworth effort which sadly never materialised.

There are some who say Coleridge gained the idea for The Rime of the Ancient Mariner, written at Nether Stowey, during a walk into North Devon with the Wordsworths. Coleridge also brought essayist and critic William Hazlitt to the Valley of the Rocks. The latter could not believe it when the poet ran out bare-headed into a thunderstorm to 'enjoy the commotion of the elements'. One can sympathise with Coleridge, however, for the sound of cracking thunder echoing through the valley is quite breathtaking.

TARKA COUNTRY

TARKA COUNTRY

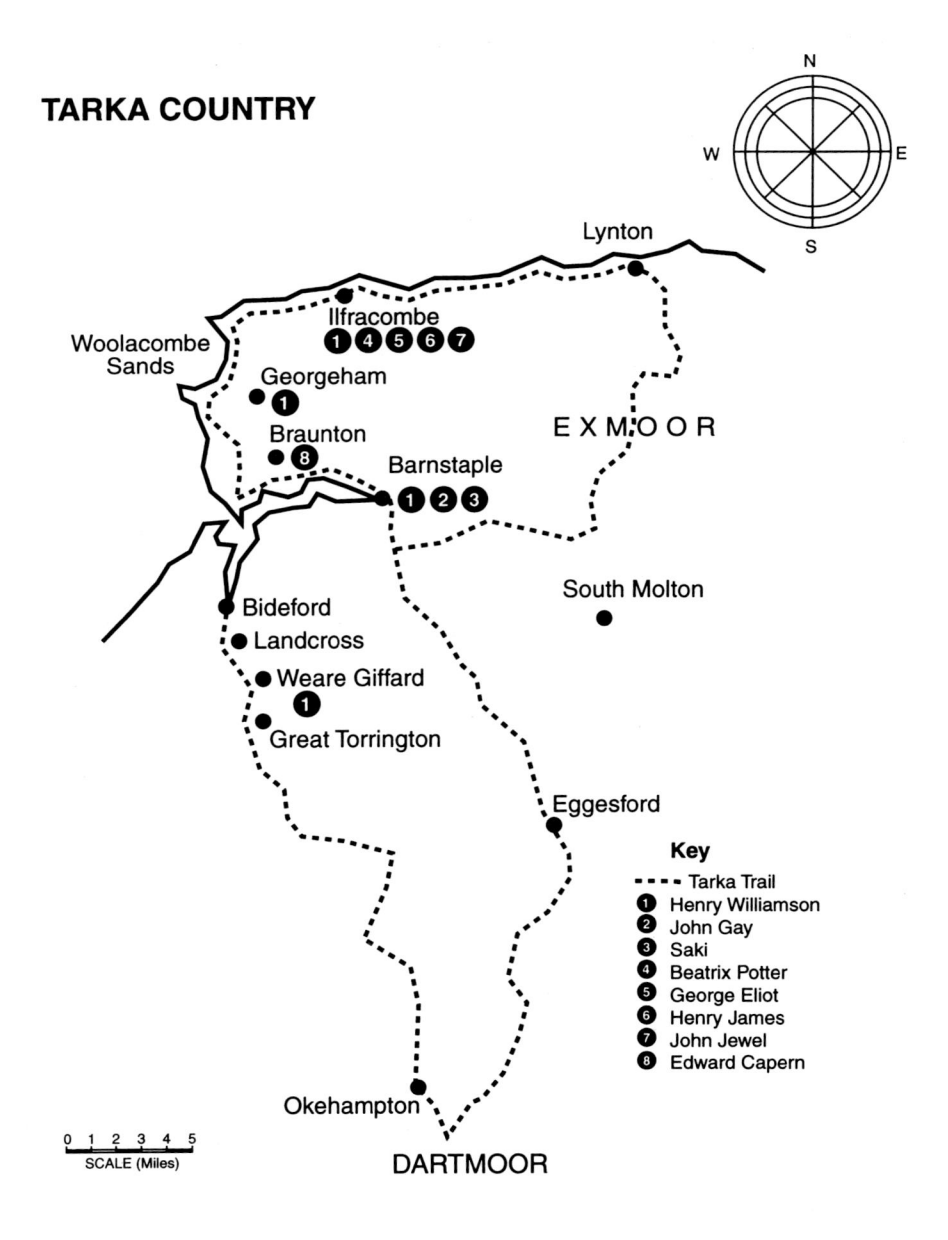

Lynton
Ilfracombe ❶❹❺❻❼
Woolacombe Sands
Georgeham ❶
E X M O O R
Braunton ❽
Barnstaple ❶❷❸
South Molton
Bideford
Landcross
Weare Giffard ❶
Great Torrington
Eggesford
Okehampton
DARTMOOR

Key
- - - - Tarka Trail
❶ Henry Williamson
❷ John Gay
❸ Saki
❹ Beatrix Potter
❺ George Eliot
❻ Henry James
❼ John Jewel
❽ Edward Capern

0 1 2 3 4 5
SCALE (Miles)

Tarka Country consists of 500 square miles of Devon countryside, ranging from the north tip of Dartmoor to the edge of Exmoor.
It is named after Henry Williamson's popular classic, Tarka the Otter.
Visitors can explore this beautiful part of the country via the Tarka Trail - a 180-mile route which follows the journey undertaken by Tarka in the book. At the centre of Tarka Country is the market town of Barnstaple, which was home to John Gay - one of the country's greatest poets.

HENRY WILLIAMSON
Novelist Henry Williamson spent most of his life in North Devon, writing about his beloved countryside.
The popular classic Tarka the Otter was published in 1927. It earned Williamson the Hawthornden Prize and propelled him to the top of his profession. He wrote other novels centred on animals, the best-known of which was Salar the Salmon, and also penned numerous short-stories.

Places to see: Tarka Trail inc Barnstaple: North Devon Museum. Weare Giffard: Canal Bridge. Landcross: Landcross Church. Shallowford. Georgeham: Skirr Cottage - Vale House - Georgeham Church - Ox's Cross. Ilfracombe: Capstone Place.

Visitors come in their droves to trace the epic journey of Williamson's best-loved character. Tarka lived - as Williamson called it - in the Land of Two Rivers. That land consists of the Taw and Torridge river valleys and now forms the heart of Tarka Country. The countryside Williamson described so beautifully has remained virtually untouched since he penned the classic novel nearly 70 years ago.
The 180-mile Tarka Trail follows the travels of Tarka in a figure of eight circle centred on Barnstaple. It covers some 500 square miles from lush mid-Devon to the spectacular north coast.
The northern loop runs along the north coast - where Williamson spent much of his life - and into Exmoor, while the southern loop stretches down to the tip of Dartmoor. The visitor is fortunate to have a number of choices as to the way they wish to explore Tarka Country.
The Tarka Trail encapsulates footpaths, cycleways and even a railway line from Barnstaple to Exeter, known as the Tarka Line. This is one of the most scenic railway journeys in the country. Completing the whole Tarka Trail is obviously difficult as it will take up longer than your visit will probably allow. This is not a problem as most people select sections of the

trail. Local tourist information centres have leaflets on the ways in which the visitor can get the best from the area.

The North Devon Museum at Barnstaple also has a display on Tarka Country, making it the perfect base from which to explore this part of the county.

The novel features real places, so the visitor, with a copy of the book and a detailed map, can literally follow Tarka's journey from his birth to death. Otters, though rare, still live in the Torridge, so you may even be fortunate enough to get a glimpse of your very own Tarka!

Tarka's journey begins and ends at Canal Bridge, which is found on the River Torridge, near Weare Giffard, at Torrington. His birthplace was a riverside holt below the bridge. The 12 trees Williamson describes in the opening scene were destroyed, but 12 new oaks and ash have since been planted as

Tarka came as far as the dramatic north coast during his epic journey.

replacements. Ironically, the death scene of Tarka for the successful film of the book was shot here on the very day Henry Williamson died!

A little further up the river is the hamlet of Landcross, home of the author's first wife. The couple were married at its tiny church in 1925. Williamson spent a lot of time here when he was planning the book.

Another place of interest on the trail is Shallowford, three miles north-west of South Molton. Williamson lived here for ten years as a tenant of Lord Fortescue, owner of the Castle Hill estate. Williamson studied salmon here for Salar the Salmon. Five of his children were brought up at the cottage by Humpy Bridge.

Part of the Tarka Trail runs along the North Devon coast where Williamson spent most of his days in Devon. He came to the county in 1921, settling in the village of Georgeham, near Braunton. He was so poor when he arrived from London it is believed he walked the 200 or so miles! The success of Tarka the Otter gave him enough money to buy a field at Ox's Cross above Georgeham. Here, he built a small hermit's hut which he used as a retreat for writing until his death in 1977. The small hut and a larger studio can still be found in the field one mile from the village. A path leading to the field crosses Pickwell Down and can be found halfway along Woolacombe Sands. It is also possible to see Skirr Cottage and Vale House, the homes Williamson occupied at Georgeham. His simple gravestone can be found in the churchyard, just yards from Skirr.

Williamson was particularly fond of Exmoor and also used it as the setting for a collection of wildlife stories published under the title, The Old Stag. One of these was a true story called Stumberleap, which followed the adventures of an ageing stag, who escaped chasing hounds by swimming across the Bristol Channel. Tarka also witnesses a stag hunt on Exmoor. Williamson, despite his love for nature and animals, was a supporter of hunting. He always said if he was an animal he would rather have a chance in the open than in an abattoir. Tarka the Otter was actually dedicated to Master of the Hunt, William Henry Rogers, who gave the author advice about otter hunts.

The author was a controversial figure who became mistrusted after praising Adolf Hitler in the foreword of the 1936 edition of The Flax of Dreams. His final years, like his early years, were sad times. He divorced his first wife and married a local woman called Christine Duffield. They bought a cottage at Capstone Place in Ilfracombe, but she, like the author's first wife, was also to leave him. Williamson spent the final few years alone at Ilfracombe. The cottage - number four - can be found under the shadow of Capstone Hill. It has a plaque informing visitors of its famous literary connection.

There are too many places of interest on the Tarka Trail to mention here. One must remember the Tarka Trail is probably the longest literary walk in the country!

Most people simply pick out their favourite part of the book and head for that location. Those lucky enough to have the time can, at a reasonable pace, complete the whole trail in about two weeks.

JOHN GAY

John Gay was a hugely-successful poet and dramatist. His most-famous work was The Beggar's Opera, which appeared four years before his death in 1732. The ballad opera was produced by John Rich, which gave vent to the famous saying that it made 'Gay rich and Rich gay'!

Places to see: Barnstaple: High Street - St Anne's Chapel - North Devon Museum.

Barnstaple - which sits at the heart of Tarka Country - was the birthplace of poet John Gay. He was born at High Street in 1685. His mother and father died when he was still a child, so the task of bringing him up was left to his uncle Thomas. Gay was educated at the local Grammar School, which was once based at St Anne's Chapel, a 14th-century building near the parish church. Its School Room still contains the desk where the young student wrote his early words of wisdom. Under the tuition of poet Robert Luck, Gay became interested in literature and developed into an accomplished student. He went to London when he finished his education and began an apprenticeship with a mercer, but soon returned when he became homesick. This time he stayed with another uncle before returning to the capital to make his name. Gay never returned to Devon, but shortly before his death he took a house near Codden Hill, south of Barnstaple, where he intended to retire. Only illness prevented him.

The North Devon Museum has a portrait of the poet. Though his house at High Street has long disappeared, visitors can find the spot thanks to a plaque on the wall of the current building at the junction with Joy Street.

Another author who was brought up in the Barnstaple area was Hector Hugh Munro - better-known as SAKI. He came to Devon in 1872 when he was just two-years-old. His mother had died, so the children were moved to Broadgate Villa in the village of Pilton, the home of his grandmother and two aunts. Hector stayed at Broadgate Villa until he was 12, when he was transferred to a school at Exmouth. The two aunts were notoriously bad-tempered and later featured in many of his short-stories, notably Sredni Vashtar, which is found in The Chronicles of Clovis, and The Lumber-Room from Beasts and Super-Beasts. On both occasions the author extracts 'revenge' on his aunts by ensuring they meet their comeuppance.

Broadgate Villa now forms two properties - Fairmead and Fairview. They can be found on the corner of Bellaire and Bellaire Drive.

Saki later had spells living with his father at Heanton Punchardon, near

Braunton, and Westward Ho! Many of his classic short-stories are set in the West Country and North Devon in particular.

Saki was also a brave soldier. His literary career was cut short when he was killed in action during the First World War.

The north coast of Devon is home to a number of popular seaside resorts. One of those is Ilfracombe, which has been blessed by a number of literary visitors over the years.

BEATRIX POTTER spent many childhood holidays in the resort.

The long flight of steps to the harbour basin in the town get a mention in The Tale of Little Pig Robinson.

GEORGE ELIOT, whose novels include Middlemarch and Silas Marner, came to Ilfracombe with George Henry Lewes in 1856. She is believed to have loved the resort.

Novelist and short-story writer HENRY JAMES was another who enjoyed holidays in this part of Devon.

George Eliot was among the many visitors to fall in love with the views of Ilfracombe.

Just over two miles east of Ilfracombe is the tiny village of Berrynarbor. Author and bishop JOHN JEWEL was born here at Bowden Farm in 1522. He became famous for his defence of the Church of England in Apologia Ecclesiae Anglicanae (Apology for the Church of England) which was written in 1562, while he was Bishop of Salisbury. Queen Elizabeth insisted it should be read in every church in the country. The parish church has a monument to Jewel.

Postman-poet EDWARD CAPERN - who lived at Bideford - spent the final few years of his life at a cottage in Braunton. He is buried in the nearby village of Heanton Punchardon. The bell he used on his round to announce his arrival was attached to his tombstone.

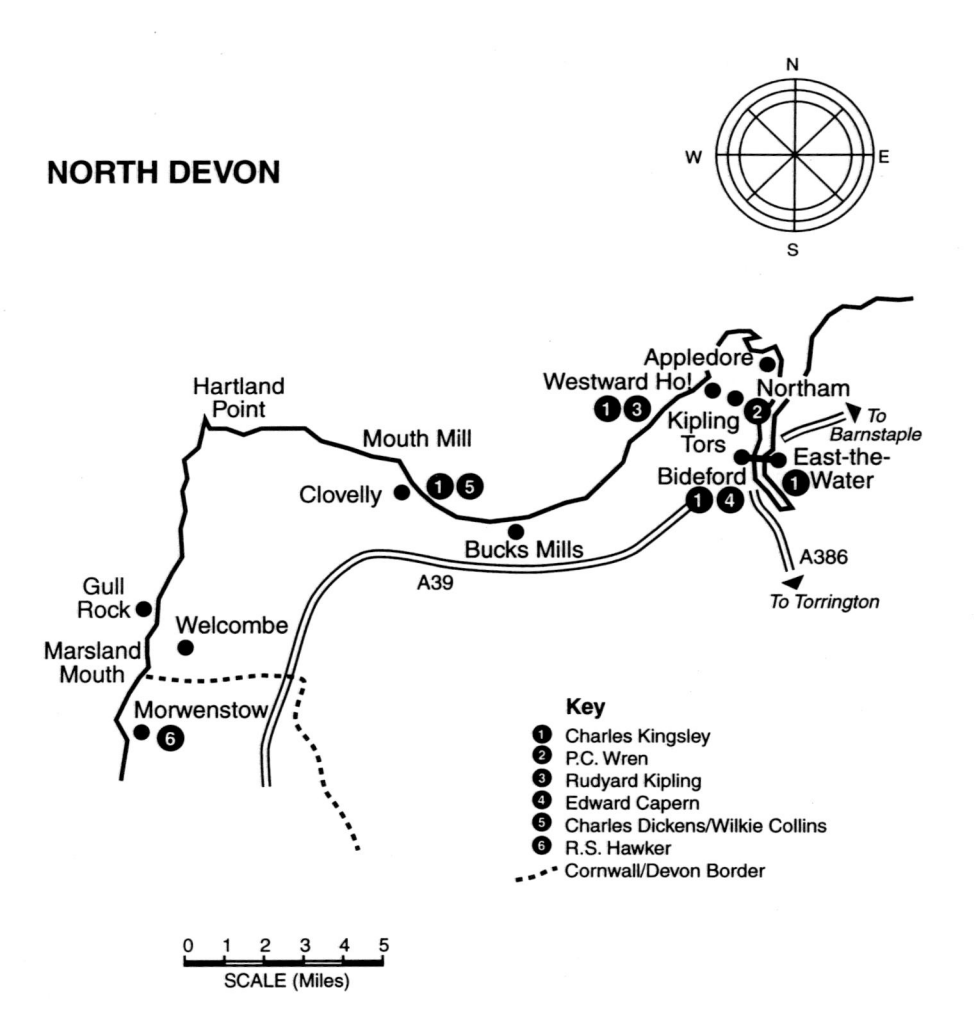

NORTH DEVON

NORTH DEVON

Key
1. Charles Kingsley
2. P.C. Wren
3. Rudyard Kipling
4. Edward Capern
5. Charles Dickens/Wilkie Collins
6. R.S. Hawker
- - - Cornwall/Devon Border

North Devon and its diverse landscape has something to inspire all kinds of writers. The coastline is home to beautiful villages such as Clovelly; busy seaside resorts such as Westward Ho! and even an historical port in the form of Bideford.

Novelist Charles Kingsley was influenced by all three of the above places and used the Bideford area as the setting for one of the country's greatest novels - Westward Ho! The resort of Westward Ho! arose from the success of the book and is named in honour of its author.

The harsh north coast is also home to one or two eerie legends, such as the legend of wrecker Cruel Coppinger, a man who would inspire the pen of any writer!

CHARLES KINGSLEY

Charles Kingsley was Dartmoor-born, but it was the north coast of Devon which played such an important part in his life. The area became the inspiration for much of his work, even though he lived outside the county for long periods.

Kingsley is best-remembered for Westward Ho! and the children's classic, The Water-Babies, which was written for his youngest son and epitomised the author's love of the sea.

Places to see: Westward Ho: Clovelly: Clovelly Church - The Red Lion - Kingsley Exhibition. Northam: Burrough House.
Bideford: Kingsley Statue - Royal Hotel.

Very few authors share the honour of having a resort named after their greatest work. Not that Charles Kingsley ever wanted Westward Ho! to be named after the epic sea adventure which made him and this part of North Devon famous. The country-loving Kingsley was appalled at the idea of a resort being built on Northam Burrows and could never bring himself to visit it. There is no doubt he was partly-responsible for its creation. The classic novel encouraged more and more people to visit the area and prompted the authorities to build a holiday base to accommodate them. Westward Ho! was officially opened in 1863 complete with all the usual seaside trappings, and despite an indifferent beginning, grew into a popular holiday destination. Strangely, Westward Ho! - apart from the name - has few monuments to the man who helped create it, though the resort is the perfect base from which to explore Kingsley Country.

Using Westward Ho! as a base the visitor is within easy reach of two places which played an important part in the life of Charles Kingsley - Clovelly and Bideford.

The sloping cliff-top village of Clovelly is found about nine miles along the coastal footpath. The walk is a delight in itself and one the author would no doubt have undertaken during his spells living in the village. The walker first has to pass over Kipling Tors, named after Rudyard Kipling, a former pupil of the United Services College at Westward Ho! The path runs above many secluded pebble beaches until it reaches the tiny village of Bucks Mills, about six miles from Westward Ho! This is the first sign of civilisation along the coast path and worthy of a stop in its own right. Clovelly is another three miles further along. Motorists should be aware no cars can enter the old-world village of Clovelly, so they must park at the Clovelly Centre, which is situated at the end of a toll road known as the Hobby Drive.

Kingsley came to Clovelly when he was 12, his father having been appointed village curate. It was here he began to dream of sea adventures and to listen to tales of heroes such as seafarer Richard Grenville - who later featured in Westward Ho! It is hardly surprising Kingsley fell in love with the charms of the village. Few visitors leave with a bad opinion of it. Kingsley best sums up Clovelly himself: 'It is as if the place had stood still while all the world had been rushing and rumbling past it.'

Clovelly has just one cobbled street which plummets towards the sea. At the bottom of the street you will find the famous harbourside pub, The Red Lion. It is a perfect place to take refreshment before the long climb back up the hill! A former landlord was Robert Yeo, who was the inspiration behind one of the novel's main characters. Clovelly also became the setting for Two Years Ago, which Kingsley wrote shortly after leaving Devon for the final time in 1855. Clovelly Church - where his father served - honours the author with a brass plaque. There is also a Kingsley Exhibition in the village. The biggest tribute to Kingsley, however, and the one which would please him most, is the fact the village has changed little from when he knew it and loved it as a boy. Of course, there are one or two more visitors to Clovelly these days - but then Kingsley himself will have to take some responsibility for that!

Further along the coast path, if you should wish to continue your journey, are a number of places featured in Westward Ho! such as Clovelly Dykes, Mouth Mill and Marsland Mouth, where Rose Salterne waded into the water at Midnight. Kingsley loved this stretch of the north coast and would regularly walk it.

The visitor should be aware it is, however, one of the most-remote parts of the county, so there is little chance of obtaining refreshment or public transport to get back!

Another fine walk from Westward Ho! is in the other direction to the town of Bideford. By road the journey is barely two miles, but the nicer route is along the coastal path through Northam Burrows and the fishing village of Appledore, which amounts to about six miles.

Northam Burrows - a country park - sits next to Westward Ho! and is sheltered by the famous Pebble Ridge. The coast path runs through it and turns inland, running along the Torridge Estuary to Bideford. Before reaching Bideford, the walker will pass the outskirts of Northam. Burrough House - the ancestral home of 16th-century navigators Stephen and William Burrough - was where Kingsley based the home of Amyas Leigh - the hero of Westward Ho!

Bideford was where Kingsley actually wrote the tale. He came to the town in 1854, lodging at Northdown Hall, a big house which stood back from the Strand. From an upstairs room, commanding a view of the shipyards, Kingsley completed his masterpiece. It took him barely seven months.

Westward Ho! was published in 1855. The original manuscript was 950 pages long. It contained a mammoth quarter of a million words and was originally published in three volumes. The book was an instant success, becoming a best-seller overnight. By the end of the century it had been reprinted 38 times!

The adventures of Amyas Leigh, most of which took place around the north coast of Devon, brought Kingsley fame and wealth. It was not his first or last work, but nothing would ever equal its success. Kingsley left Bideford and Devon for the final time after the publication of Westward Ho!

The town has many lasting reminders of its most-famous resident. A statue of Kingsley can be found on the Quay at the entrance to Victoria Park. The Quay was also home to the former Ship Inn where the lovers of the ill-fated 'Rose of Torridge' formed their Brotherhood. It is now a restaurant. Across the river, which can be crossed via Bideford Bridge, is East-the-Water. Kingsley briefly lodged at the Royal Hotel when he first arrived before taking up residence at Northdown Hall. It is believed he penned part of Westward Ho! here. The hotel has dedicated a room to the author.

Burrough House at Northam, where Kingsley based the Leigh family, does have another literary connection. Novelist P.C. WREN was born at the house in 1885. He is remembered for the classic Beau Geste - a tale of three brothers who leave England to serve in the French Foreign Legion. Wren set the home of the Gestes in Devon and may have based it on Burrough.

The original Burrough House, which Kingsley would have known, was pulled down in 1868 and two new houses were built on the site. Burrough House and Burrough Farm are privately-owned and not open to the public.

RUDYARD KIPLING

Westward Ho! was also home to novelist and poet Rudyard Kipling during his teenage years. Bombay-born Kipling made a name for himself as a caustic observer of Anglo-Indian society and became the unofficial spokesman for the British Empire. His novels included the hugely-successful Kim and The Jungle Book. His poems, including the collection Barrack-Room Ballads, were just as popular. Kipling's famous, If, was voted the nation's favourite poem in a recent survey.

Charles Kingsley is honoured at Bideford, the setting for his classic, Westward Ho!

Places to see: Westward Ho!: Kipling Terrace - Kipling Tors.

Rudyard Kipling spent a relatively happy four years at Westward Ho! He came to the resort in 1878 to attend the former United Services College. The college was set up for sons of servicemen to prepare them for a military career. Kipling, having spent his early years in India, had been sent to England to be educated. He was just 12 when he arrived at Westward Ho! The headmaster at the time of his arrival was Cormell Price - a friend of the family. He gave the young Rudyard a free-run of his extensive library - an offer taken up with relish. It was during this time Kipling began to read poetry and put pen to paper himself. Kipling stayed for four years, leaving when he was 16 to take up a post as an assistant editor for a military newspaper in Lahore.

The United Services College no longer exists, though the visitor should have no trouble finding the spot where it once stood. Kipling Terrace - named after the author - has a plaque which marks the spot. This is the perfect place to begin a short walk to a quieter part of the resort - one Kipling regularly took himself.

The gorse-covered hills of Kipling Tors, now owned by the National Trust, can be found less than a mile away. These beautiful 18 acres were named in memory of the author, as it was reputed to be his favourite spot. He would regularly get away from his hectic school life to enjoy the peace and tranquillity of the hills. It still is a wonderful place from which to draw inspiration and one can see how easily the young Rudyard would have been inspired by it.

Sadly, there are few other Kipling memorials to be found at Westward Ho! these days. Most visitors are too busy enjoying its many other attractions to notice them, anyway!

The best way to discover Kipling's Westward Ho! is to read his 1899 book Stalky & Co, which drew on his experiences at the United Services College. Kipling actually dedicated the book to his old headmaster. The book features the tales of three students - Stalky, M'Turk and Beetle. The latter is based on the author.

North Devon was also the stamping ground of postman-poet EDWARD CAPERN - a man of words as well as letters! His first-class service to residents included a song and a smile and earned him the nickname, The Postman-Poet of Bideford. He would frequently recite songs and poems during his daily round - a 13-mile round trip from Bideford to the village of Buckland Brewer. It was not just the locals who were treated to his work, either. Lord Palmerston was so impressed with Capern's famous battle-song, The Lion Flag of England, he gave him £40 a year from the Civil List to fund his writing. Palmerston said Capern's patriotic poems had given him hope and strength to bear some of the country's greatest trials.

Capern became well-known throughout the literary world and various distinguished authors such as Kingsley, Tennyson and Dickens all wrote to him at his home in Mill Street. Capern spent his latter life at a cottage in Braunton. He was buried in the churchyard at nearby Heanton Punchardon. CHARLES DICKENS was another writer mesmerised by the charms of Clovelly. He came to this part of the county in 1861 with fellow-writer and close friend WILKIE COLLINS. The latter, famous for The Woman in White and The Moonstone, helped Dickens write A Message from the Sea, in which Clovelly was referred to as Steepway. Visitors will not be surprised by the name. Clovelly is so steep in places, the bottom of some houses almost touch the roof of the next!

A Message from the Sea is found in Dickens' Christmas Stories.

The remaining stretch of the north coast, to the border with Cornwall, as mentioned earlier, is one of the remotest parts of the country. It is therefore surprising it holds any literary connections at all! The area was, however, made famous by the eccentric poet and vicar R.S. HAWKER. He would regularly cross the Devon border from his Morwenstow vicarage. He was appointed curate of Welcombe in 1850 and often made the short journey to St Nectan's Church on his pony. Welcombe sits just inside the Devon border. It is a fine place to begin a walk to the cliff-side Morwenstow Church - a mere three miles away. Hawker would make the journey while he sang hymns at the top of his voice. This was to frighten evil spirits, as he was convinced a demon leapt in front of him on one occasion!

It is no surprise Charles Dickens referred to Clovelly as Steepway.

The North Devon coast around Welcombe was also the stamping ground of legendary wrecker Cruel Coppinger. Coppinger, who later became a subject of Hawker's pen, led an amazing life. He caused havoc in the parish of Hartland with his evil ways and gave chasing customs officers a torrid time. His demise was as dramatic as his life had been. With the officers closing in on him he decided to flee the area for good. He was spotted one night on top of Gull Rock, near Marsland Mouth, signalling to a boat. The vessel came and took him away, but as the boat sailed into the distance, a storm blew up and it was lost forever. There were many who claimed Coppinger's victims had finally gained their revenge!

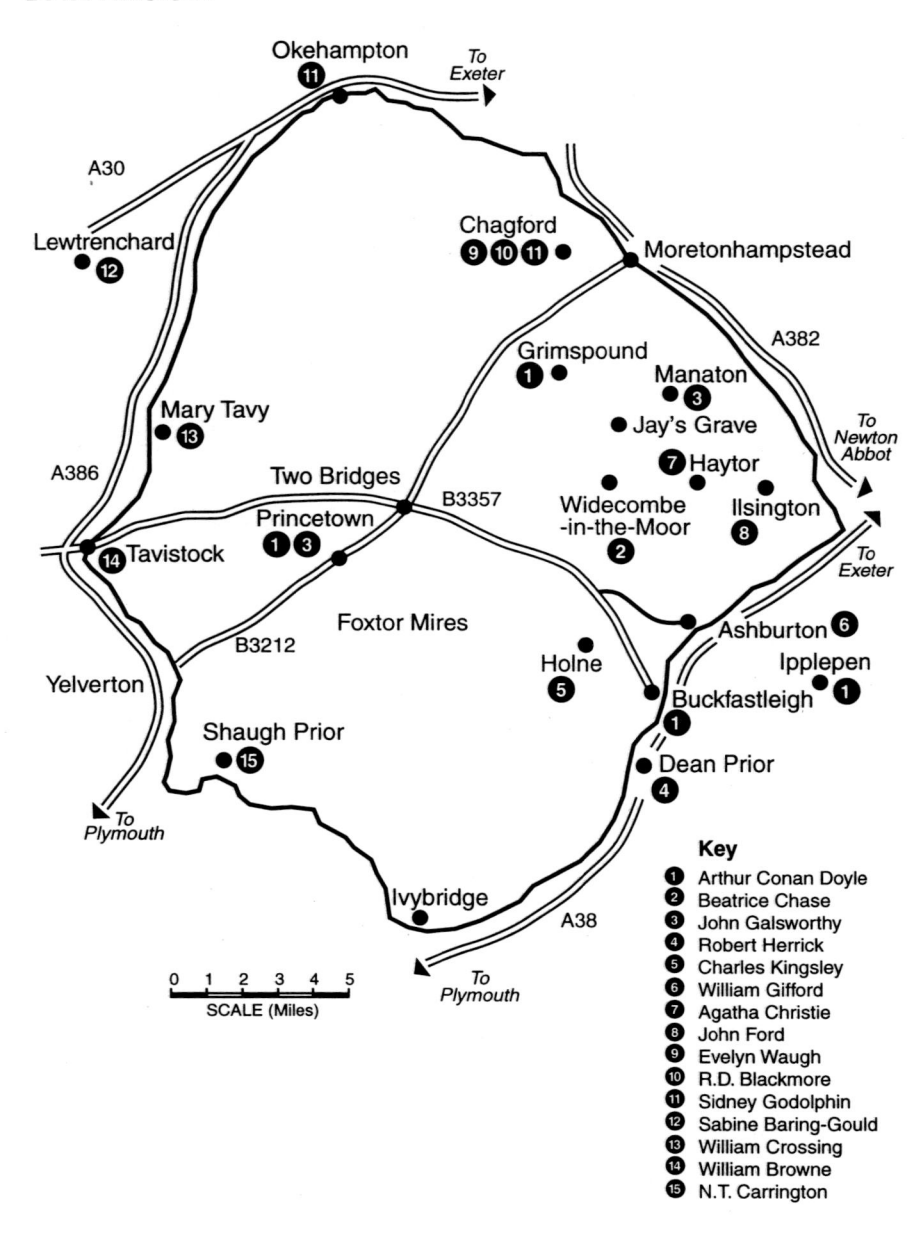

DARTMOOR

DARTMOOR

Key
1. Arthur Conan Doyle
2. Beatrice Chase
3. John Galsworthy
4. Robert Herrick
5. Charles Kingsley
6. William Gifford
7. Agatha Christie
8. John Ford
9. Evelyn Waugh
10. R.D. Blackmore
11. Sidney Godolphin
12. Sabine Baring-Gould
13. William Crossing
14. William Browne
15. N.T. Carrington

Dartmoor has often been described as the last true wilderness in Southern England. It is therefore not surprising the area has attracted numerous writers. Its dramatic and often eerie terrain has been immortalised through a number of works. The best-known is Arthur Conan Doyle's classic mystery, The Hound of the Baskervilles.

Many other writers, such as novelist John Galsworthy, have come to live in the peaceful surroundings in their bid for solitude. Dartmoor has remained virtually untouched for centuries and the visitor will see exactly what the writer saw.

Dartmoor National Park covers 365 square miles, so it is impossible to cover every inch enjoyed by writers. The visitor should also be aware there is very little public transport, so a car or a good pair of walking boots is a necessity!

ARTHUR CONAN DOYLE

Arthur Conan Doyle became one of the most-popular authors of his time. Sherlock Holmes, his greatest creation, is known and loved throughout the world. The detective's most-famous case - The Hound of the Baskervilles - brought him to remote and wild Dartmoor.

Places to see: Princetown: High Moorland Visitor Centre - Dartmoor Prison. Foxtor Mires. Grimspound.
Buckfastleigh: Holy Trinity Church.   Ipplepen: Park Hill House.

Going on the trail of Sherlock Holmes is not easy as Doyle was inspired by almost every region of Dartmoor when he penned The Hound of the Baskervilles. The best place to begin a tour is at Princetown - the highest town in England. Its High Moorland Visitor Centre contains a tribute to Arthur Conan Doyle and Sherlock Holmes, giving tourists all the necessary background information on the area's famous literary connection. Doyle actually stayed at the centre when it was the Old Duchy Hotel in order to carry out research for the book.

Just over the road from the Visitor Centre is The Devil's Elbow pub. Its sign also does its best to remind people of the Holmes connection.

Princetown's most-famous tourist attraction - though it is fortunately only open to a select few - is the imposing Dartmoor Prison. The prison featured in the book, when the servants of the Baskervilles signal to an escaped prisoner. The Great Grimpen Mire, where the tale is set, is believed to be based on Foxtor Mires, which is situated about two-and-a-half miles from Princetown. The area is one of the most-desolate parts of the moor. Walkers wishing to soak up its eerie atmosphere should take warning. Doyle did not choose to base the book on its mist-covered tors and bogs for no reason! An Ordnance Survey map and compass are vital tools for anyone wishing to walk any of Dartmoor's remoter parts.

Doyle was also inspired by other parts of the moor. Grimspound is situated three miles north of Widecombe-in-the-Moor. In the book, Sherlock Holmes uses the remnants of a hut in a prehistoric settlement as a hideout. Doyle's model was the ancient village of Grimspound. The four-acre area, surrounded by a circular nine-foot thick wall, houses the remains of 24 circular huts. Traces of doorways and fireplaces are still visible. It is the finest example of a Bronze Age settlement found on the moor and well worth a visit.

The Devil's Elbow Pub at Princetown.

Doyle's inspiration for the book's characters are believed to have come from the other side of the moor. Buckfastleigh, a small town on the edge of South-East Dartmoor, was the home of Squire Richard Cabell.

The hill-top Holy Trinity Church contains the remains of the evil 17th-century squire, who according to legend, sold his soul to the Devil. When he died a large stone slab was placed over his tomb and a stone porch was built around it in order to stop him rising as an evil spirit. Locals claimed the Hounds of Hell gathered around the tomb on the night he was buried and began howling when they realised he could not get out. Stories of their piercing, haunting cries fired the imagination of Doyle when he was told the story during a visit to the area with friends. The tomb can easily be picked out in the churchyard.

It is claimed Doyle penned most of the novel while staying at Park Hill House in Ipplepen, which is situated on the outskirts of the moor, near Newton Abbot. The house belonged to his friend Fletcher-Robinson - to whom he dedicated the book. It is believed Doyle changed the name of Cabell to Baskerville after a coachmen employed here. The house is not open to the public.

There are also many other claims to the origin of The Hound of the Baskervilles, so it is probable we shall never know exactly what gave Doyle the idea. It is perhaps fitting so much mystery surrounds one of the greatest mysteries ever to be written!

The tomb of Squire Richard Cabell - the inspiration behind Arthur Conan Doyle's, The Hound of the Baskervilles.

BEATRICE CHASE

The work of Dartmoor author Beatrice Chase is little-known today, but she was one of the most-interesting writers ever to put pen to paper. Her home village was beautiful Widecombe-in-the-Moor, which is worth a visit any day of the year.

Places to see: Widecombe-in-the-Moor: Widecombe Church - Venton House. Jay's Grave.

The eccentric Dartmoor author is responsible for a tradition, which like her work, has never been forgotten. Beatrice Chase - her real name was Olive Katharine Parr - is thought to have been the first person to secretly place fresh flowers on Jay's Grave. The unusually-located grave is situated within easy reach of the village. It can be found on the roadside near Hound Tor, which is less than two miles from Widecombe. Though its inhabitant died about 200 years ago, the grave is still one of Dartmoor's most-popular attractions because of the romantic legend associated with it. Tragic Kitty Jay was a simple workhouse girl who lived at a farm in Manaton. She committed suicide after being seduced by the farmer's son. Like other suicides she was denied a burial in consecrated ground and was interred at a crossroads after having a stake thrust through her heart. The grave was excavated in the mid-19th century to discover if the legend was true, and sure enough, the bones of a young woman were found. Kitty was re-buried in a coffin and her grave restored. Touched by the story, Beatrice began placing fresh flowers on the grave when she moved to the village and Venton House at the beginning of the century.

Strangely, the tradition continued even after her death in 1955, though mystery still surrounds who took up the job. Even today visitors will find fresh flowers at the lonely resting place. Beatrice will be remembered for her eccentricity, but her books and poetry also contained beautiful and lasting descriptions of her beloved moor. Her plain cross in Widecombe Churchyard contains the simple inscription: Pray for Olive Katharine Parr.

The grave of Beatrice Chase - alias Olive Katharine Parr - can be found at Widecombe Church.

Venton House still stands and can be found on the outskirts of the village half a mile on from the Rugglestone Inn.

Beatrice, with her strange ways, became the subject of a book herself, when John Oxenham penned, My Lady of the Moor. More recently, local author Judy Chard also wrote The Mysterious Lady of the Moor, the life story of Beatrice Chase.

The work of Beatrice Chase is becoming more and more popular these days and will no doubt, like the legend of Jay's Grave, live on for many more years to come.

JOHN GALSWORTHY

Novelist John Galsworthy is best-remembered for The Forsyte Saga.

He spent most of his life in the South East, but had his roots firmly in Devon - the home of his ancestors. He spent many happy years residing at a farm on the edge of Dartmoor.

Places to see: Manaton: Wingstone Farm. Jay's Grave.
Princetown: Dartmoor Prison.

Novelist and playwright John Galsworthy fell in love with Dartmoor and enjoyed many summers here. He spent his honeymoon at Wingstone Farm in the quiet village of Manaton and returned over a number of years as a summer tenant. George Bernard Shaw, Joseph Conrad and W.H. Hudson were among the many literary visitors to the farm.

Wingstone is not open to the public, but can be viewed from the road which runs through the village. It is situated in sight of the lovely parish church a few hundred yards away. Galsworthy also had a fine view of Bowerman's Nose, which is situated on a hill to the rear of Wingstone. The walk up to the unusual set of rocks is one which Galsworthy, like many others, would no doubt have undertaken. It is well worth the climb for the splendid views it affords.

Another visitor to Wingstone was Harley Granville-Barker, who produced the author's famous play, The Silver Box, in 1906. Galsworthy also wrote part of The Country House and Fraternity while at Wingstone. The author would often sit in the garden with a pad on his knee. He loved the area and its people and was known for his generosity. On occasions he helped out elderly neighbours who could not afford their high rents by buying their cottages and halving the rent himself! Neighbours would often see the author riding around the moor on his horse, with his pet dog running by his side. You too will have no difficulty imagining the sound of clicking hooves along the delightful Manaton lanes.

The surrounding area and its people had a great influence on Galsworthy. The Moor Grave and The Apple Tree were based on the story of Kitty Jay, the tragic suicide who occupies Jay's Grave, near Widecombe-in-the-Moor. Jay's Grave is a mere two miles from Manaton. Galsworthy's love for the area is also recalled in Life and Letters.

John Galsworthy often walked through the imposing entrance of Dartmoor Prison.

The author also journeyed to bleak Dartmoor Prison at Princetown on several occasions, while campaigning for the rights of prisoners. His 1910 play Justice helped force through new legislation which reduced solitary confinement in English prisons.

ROBERT HERRICK

Poet Robert Herrick spent a large portion of his life on the edge of Dartmoor at Dean Prior, near Buckfastleigh. Though he lived in Devon for 34 years, the county never won his heart and he directed much of his bitterness towards his neighbours.

Herrick's most-successful work was the collection, Hesperides, which consisted of more than 1,000 poems, hymns and songs.

Places to see: Dean Prior: Church of St George the Martyr.

The church and parsonage where Robert Herrick spent much of his life sits on the busy A38 road. The rush of traffic these days has all but destroyed the peace and solitude Herrick must have experienced when appointed to the living of Dean Prior in 1629. Not that Herrick would have complained, for he actually found the area too dull! He had been enjoying life in London with literary friends such as Ben Jonson and described his new home in Devon as being a place of banishment. He wrote home to say he had never been so sad and discontent in all his life. His frustration was often taken out on locals. The area and its people inspired much of his work, but he was rarely complimentary. He once described his parishioners as being like rude savages! Herrick was freed from his 'banishment' in 1647 when he was dismissed from Dean Prior because of his Royalist sympathies. He penned a farewell poem to the parish and returned to London.

Fortunately - or perhaps unfortunately - Herrick was reinstated after the Restoration in 1662 and returned to the area he so loathed. He spent the

Robert Herrick would walk this very path to reach his church and 'savages'.

remainder of his life with his servant Prewdence Baldwin. He did not write any more poems and died in 1674, a quiet and lonely man. He was buried in an unmarked grave. Visitors to the church today will see parishioners have forgiven the controversial poet. It contains a number of memorials, including a window and tablet. There is also an epitaph to Prewdence. A simple slate

has since been placed in the churchyard to compensate for the lack of tombstone.
The Old Parsonage is situated beside the church facing the main road.
It is easy to imagine the disgruntled Herrick trudging the few yards into church to face his 'savages'!

There are many more Dartmoor literary connections worth investigating. CHARLES KINGSLEY is best-known in North Devon, but Dartmoor also played an important part in his life. He was born in the village of Holne, which is situated a mere three miles from Buckfastleigh, and spent the first six weeks of his life here.
Kingsley often believed his love of nature and the Devon countryside was instilled into him by his mother - even before his birth! She loved the countryside and would regularly walk from Holne Rectory to Leigh Tor. Her rambles continued even when she was pregnant as she was convinced she could transfer her love of the surroundings to the unborn child in the womb.
The walk from Holne Rectory to Leigh Tor - about a mile in length - takes the walker along the River Dart for part of the trek. One can still see why Mrs Kingsley so enjoyed her daily walk! Holne Church has a stained glass window in memory of Kingsley.
Also in this part of South-East Dartmoor is the market town of Ashburton. This is a perfect base from which to explore this part of the moor.
It was also home to satirist WILLIAM GIFFORD - the man once partly-blamed for the death of John Keats. Gifford, who spent his early life at Ashburton, became the first editor of the controversial Quarterly Review in 1809. Romantic poet Robert Southey accused Gifford and the magazine of treating writers with the same respect fishermen treated worms!
For a long time people blamed Gifford and the publication for the untimely death of Keats. The editor agreed to publish John Wilson Croker's scathing review of the poet's Endymion. It was said the review so alarmed the sensitive Keats, it made him ill and speeded his demise! Fortunately, Gifford seems to have been forgiven and is today remembered as one of the country's leading satirists of his time.
Gifford was born at Ashburton in 1756 and spent a torrid childhood in the town. After the death of his parents, he was entrusted to his godfather who, despite public opinion that Gifford was intelligent enough for a promising school career, lost hope and apprenticed him to a local shoemaker. Gifford secretly learnt algebra and verses in between repairing shoes until his master found out and destroyed his books. Fortunately, there were others who sensed

the youngster had potential. Local surgeon William Cookesley got together with some friends to buy his apprenticeship to allow him to continue to study at Ashburton Grammar School. Gifford, who gained fame in the mid-1790s with the Baviad and the Maeviad - tales which scoffed at the pretences of a contemporary group of poets - never forgot the surgeon who helped make his name and left £25,000 to his son after his own death in 1826.

There are few monuments to Gifford. Ashburton Grammar School no longer exists, though visitors can visit St Lawrence's Chapel, where it was once based. The chapel was built in the 14th century and was gradually turned into a school. Only the tower of the chapel remains. Visitors should be aware it is only open during the summer. Ashburton Museum - also only open during the summer season - is another place to discover more on the life of the town's most-famous son.

South Devon crime writer AGATHA CHRISTIE was another who loved Dartmoor and used it as a retreat. She stayed at the Moorland Hotel, Haytor, for two weeks to complete her first book - The Mysterious Affair at Styles. She loved the remote moor and would regularly come here in search of inspiration. Dartmoor featured in a number of her books. The Sittaford Mystery was named after Sittaford Tor and set in a snow-bound Dartmoor village. Agatha conceived the story after a heavy snow storm. The moor also appears in Evil Under the Sun and The Big Four.

On the outskirts of Newton Abbot, on the edge of the moor, is the village of Ilsington. This was the birthplace of dramatist JOHN FORD. He was born at Bagtor House and baptised in the parish church in 1586. He spent his early childhood years in the village before moving to London. Little is known about his life - especially after 1639 when he vanished from London. It is possible he returned to Devon to see out his final days in the county. There are some who suggest he returned to Bagtor House to die. His plays include the tragedies, The Broken Heart and 'Tis Pity She's a Whore.

The moorland town of Chagford is also well worth a visit as it has at least three literary connections.

EVELYN WAUGH penned the popular novel Brideshead Revisited in the town in 1944. He often used the Easton Court Hotel as a retreat and a place to write.

The church at Chagford has a memorial to bride Mary Whiddon, who was shot by a jealous lover as she left the building in 1641. This tragic tale is believed to have been the basis for the dramatic altar-shooting in Lorna Doone, though R.D. BLACKMORE gave his incident a happy ending. Blackmore also set his novel, Christowell, on Dartmoor.

Most visitors to Chagford come for another sombre claim to fame.

The Three Crowns Inn is reputed to be where Cavalier poet SIDNEY GODOLPHIN was killed during the Civil War in 1643. He received a mortal shot by a musket just above the knee and died instantly. He was buried at All Saints' Church in Okehampton.

About nine miles from Okehampton, just off the busy A30 to Launceston, is the village of Lewtrenchard. Novelist and hymn-writer SABINE BARING-GOULD spent 43 years here as squire and rector. He is best-remembered for the hymn, Onward, Christian Soldiers, but his list of work is never-ending and includes a number of novels, poems and non-fiction books. He was still writing up to the day he died at the age of 89.

Royalist poet Sidney Godolphin was shot and killed within the porch at the Three Crowns Inn, Chagford.

A visit to the village church he served is well worth the effort. His father was squire of the 3,000 acres of Lewtrenchard and Sabine inherited it all upon his father's death in 1872. He became rector nine years later on his own nomination.

Sabine Baring-Gould was an expert on West Country folklore and legends, and was partly-responsible for bringing the eccentric R.S. Hawker of Morwenstow to the public's attention.

A few old legends surround the rector himself. Some say he did most of his writing standing up and had so many children did not personally know them by name! He was buried in the churchyard after his death in 1924.

Plymouth-born WILLIAM CROSSING is honoured as the greatest authority on Dartmoor of all time. He provided a complete record of every tor, hill, river and track in his celebrated Guide to Dartmoor. Crossing wrote the book while living at a cottage in Mary Tavy, on the outskirts of the moor, near Tavistock. A memorial tablet can be seen from the roadside on the wall of the cottage now called Crossings. The cottage is situated on the edge of the village on the A386 road. Unfortunately, the house is privately-owned and not open to the public. Crossing's guide was, and is still, known as the Dartmoor Bible.

The pleasant town of Tavistock was also the birthplace of 16th-century pastoral poet WILLIAM BROWNE. He was educated at the town's Grammar School before leaving the county and making his name. His famous Britannia's Pastoral - published in three volumes - featured much of the surrounding countryside.

Plymouth poet N.T. CARRINGTON is best-known for his Dartmoor poem. He is fondly remembered in the moorland village of Shaugh Prior, which is situated on the edge of South-West Dartmoor. The church has a memorial. His many admirers also created their own monument by carving his name on the famous Dewerstone, a rock overlooking the River Plym at Dewer Stone Hill close to Shaugh Bridge.

Others to write about Dartmoor include novelist EDEN PHILLPOTTS. There were many who believed he did for Devon what Thomas Hardy did for Dorset. His famous Dartmoor novels - celebrated in 20 volumes to form Dartmoor Cycle - were certainly celebrated in and out of the county. The 18 novels and two short-stories were written over a period of 25 years from 1898 to 1923. Each novel was set in a particular region of Dartmoor, the most famous being Widecombe Fair and The Secret Woman.

Phillpotts used a total of 434 characters in Dartmoor Cycle, many of which were based on real people using their real names. He presented people as he found them and described the area in minute detail. His ashes were scattered on the moor - the area which made him famous - when he died at the grand old age of 98.

Dartmoor also became the inspiration for the 1929 L.A.G. STRONG novel Dewer Rides.

PLYMOUTH AND SOUTH DEVON

**PLYMOUTH &
SOUTH DEVON**

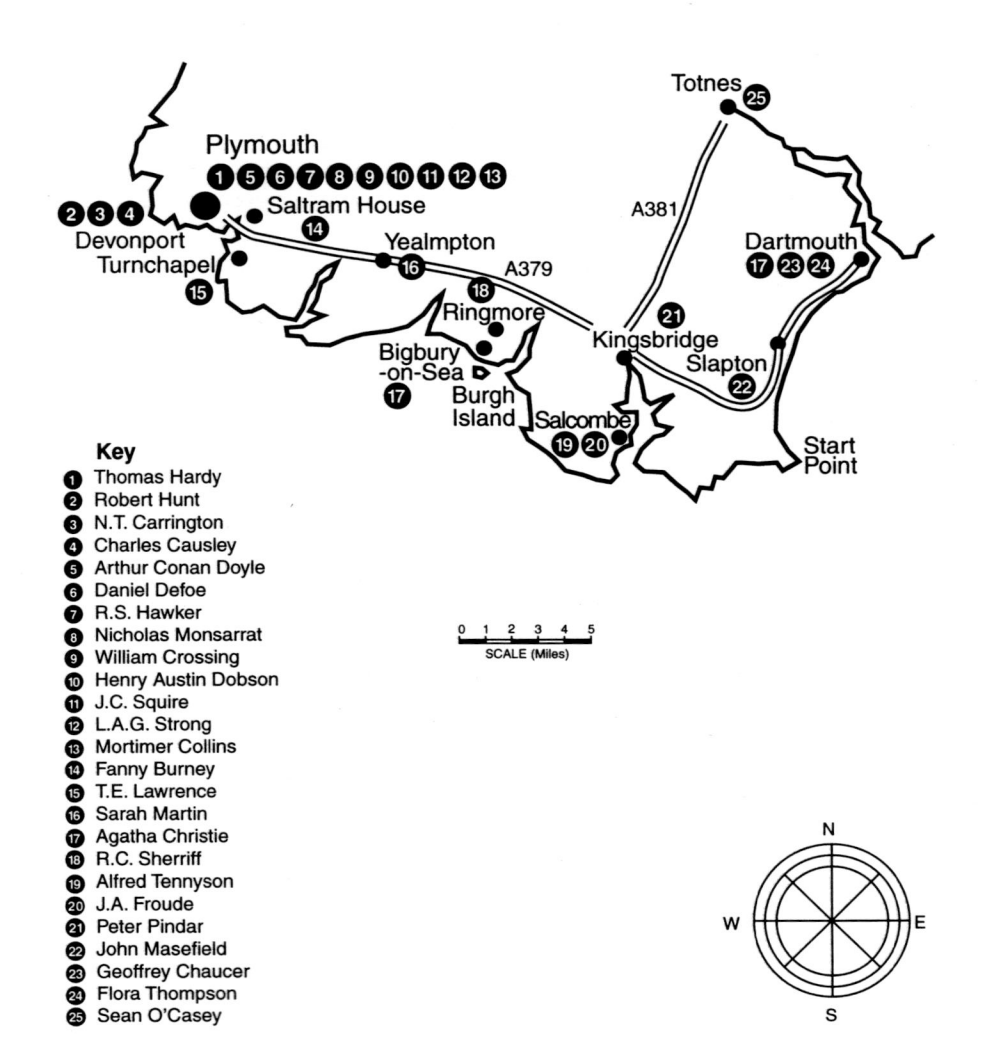

Key
1. Thomas Hardy
2. Robert Hunt
3. N.T. Carrington
4. Charles Causley
5. Arthur Conan Doyle
6. Daniel Defoe
7. R.S. Hawker
8. Nicholas Monsarrat
9. William Crossing
10. Henry Austin Dobson
11. J.C. Squire
12. L.A.G. Strong
13. Mortimer Collins
14. Fanny Burney
15. T.E. Lawrence
16. Sarah Martin
17. Agatha Christie
18. R.C. Sherriff
19. Alfred Tennyson
20. J.A. Froude
21. Peter Pindar
22. John Masefield
23. Geoffrey Chaucer
24. Flora Thompson
25. Sean O'Casey

Being a reborn city - much of Plymouth was destroyed during the Second World War - there is little physical evidence of the many writers who once lived here. There are, however, still some areas of the city which have remained untouched for centuries. The Barbican - one of those places - has more than a few tales to tell, being the departure point of The Pilgrim Fathers, Francis Drake, Walter Raleigh and other great seafarers.

The city's most-famous literary visitor was Thomas Hardy. He wrote many of his famous Love Poems here.

Famous literary connections can be found all along the south coast of Devon - one of the most-beautiful parts of the West Country.

THOMAS HARDY

Novelist and poet Thomas Hardy became one of the country's best-loved authors. His stories of rural English life still captivate readers throughout the world. It was the novel Far From the Madding Crowd which set him on the road to fame and fortune.

Plymouth was the birthplace of Hardy's first wife, Emma Gifford, herself an accomplished writer.

Places to see: Plymouth: Plymouth Railway Station - The Hoe - Sussex Street - St Andrew's Church - Charles Church - Bedford Terrace.

Thomas Hardy experienced a total contrast of emotions during two quite different visits to Plymouth. The city became a place to celebrate - and later became a place to despair! The thrill of seeing his greatest novel in print for the first time was enjoyed here, but the city - being the home of his first wife - became a place to grieve after her untimely death in 1912.

Our tour of Hardy's Plymouth begins at Plymouth Railway Station - scene of a happier moment in his life. The young architect had to change trains here when he travelled from his Dorset home to the north coast of Cornwall to work on the restoration of St Juliot Church. It was while working at the church he met and fell in love with the rector's sister-in-law - Emma Lavinia Gifford.

It was as he returned from St Juliot on New Year's Eve 1873, he noticed a billboard advertising the Cornhill Magazine and its first instalment of Far From the Madding Crowd. The excited young author bought a copy and walked the short distance to Plymouth Hoe to sit and read the opening of his greatest novel. He had already written three novels, but Far From the Madding Crowd was the book which made his name.

The Hoe offers superb views out to sea and has plenty of places to rest your weary feet. It is easy to imagine the proud young author, sitting alone on a bench, enjoying the reward of his labours.

Sadly, Hardy never saw Emma in her home town. She left when she was 18 and the couple never returned together. It was something he regretted after her sudden death. It prompted the grief-stricken writer to make a pilgrimage to Plymouth to visit the places where she grew up. How different he must have felt from all those happy visits on the way to St Juliot!

Emma was born at 10 York Street. The house and street no longer exist. This part of the city was so badly destroyed by German bombs it was swept away in the post-war rebuilding programme. Emma left York Street at an early age and spent most of her childhood at a house in Sussex Street, which is situated opposite Hoe Park off Citadel Road, immediately north of Plymouth Hoe. The street still exists, though the house - number nine - was also destroyed during the war. The house once overlooked the slopes of the Hoe. Hardy described the house with its large garden in the poem During Wind and Rain. Emma was baptised at St Andrew's Church, the premier church of Plymouth. The Gifford family regularly attended services. Emma also put her musical talents to good use and often played the organ here. The church was also gutted by bombs, with only the shell and tower surviving. Extensive repairs were carried out after the war. The church can be found just off Royal Parade at the heart of the city centre.

Another church frequented by the Giffords was Charles Church. It was also hit by bombs and all that remains today is its shell. It sits in the middle of a busy roundabout at Charles Cross, a few hundred yards from St Andrew's Church.

Hardy, during his pilgrimage to Plymouth, designed a memorial tablet in honour of Emma and arranged to have it placed in the church where she was organist.

The poet poured out his grief in a number of poems about Emma and Plymouth. They were collected under the title of Poems of 1912-13, but were better known as Hardy's Love Poems. Places, pictures the young Emma in bed listening to the bells of St Andrew's Church, while The West-of-Wessex Girl mourns the fact the couple never saw each other in Plymouth. Lonely Days was believed to be written from Emma's memoirs, while The Marble-streeted Town is a poem about Plymouth itself. All the poems were written in the city just months after Emma's death.

The only childhood home of Emma still standing can be found north of the city at Bedford Terrace, now a cul-de-sac off North Hill, north of Drake

Circus. It was again house number nine where the Giffords resided. The family were also known to have lived at properties in Courtenhay Street and Buckland Street, though the numbers are not known.

Hardy brought Elfride Swancourt and Henry Knight in A Pair of Blue Eyes into Devon. They enjoyed a boat trip along the south coast. The county was Hardy's Lower Wessex.

As mentioned earlier, Plymouth has little physical evidence of the many writers who once worked here. It is, however, well worth a visit.

Our literary tour of the city, which can be combined with a tour of Hardy's Plymouth, begins on the western side of the city at Devonport and its famous dockyard. Though not particularly pretty, this part of the city, with its warships and cargo vessels, can not be described as boring.

Devonport was the birthplace of ROBERT HUNT in 1807. He will always be remembered for his mining literature and for establishing the Miners Association of Cornwall and Devonshire, which provided classes for the education of working miners.

Plymouth-born N.T. CARRINGTON was another who knew Devonport well. He spent most of his early life here as a dock worker, but became disillusioned with his work and ran away to sea, where he was to witness the Battle of Cape St Vincent. When he returned to the city, he settled for a quieter life as a teacher and took to writing poetry and guides. It was his famous Dartmoor poem which earned him fame, but it also earned him the title of the teacher who forgot to hand in his homework! Carrington missed the chance of the 1826 prize for the Royal Society of Literature because he was unaware the closing date for entries had passed. The tale did not have an unhappy ending, however, for his efforts were rewarded by King George IV. He so liked the poem he awarded Carrington 50 guineas. It proved adequate compensation for the poet, who had to publish his work by subscription.

Cornish poet CHARLES CAUSLEY, one of the country's finest 20th-century poets, wrote about Devonport in Underneath the Water. One of his collections is also named after Union Street - the main road which leads to Devonport from Plymouth City Centre.

ARTHUR CONAN DOYLE was another who knew and loved Plymouth. He had his first taste of the county in 1882 when he accepted an offer to join the Plymouth practice of former fellow medical student George Budd. The eccentric Dr Budd had made quite a name for himself during the short space of time he had been operating a surgery at Durnford Street, in the Stonehouse area of the city. His unconventional and unscrupulous methods fascinated Doyle. People flocked to the surgery from miles around to take up his revolutionary offer of 'free consultations but pay for your medicine'. It was no surprise Budd issued drugs indiscriminately!

The public loved him, however. The waiting room was sometimes so overcrowded the queue often extended to the hall and staircase. Budd pushed patients around and continuously shouted and joked with them. Doyle described the practice at full swing as being as funny as any pantomime! Doyle was given his own room but usually ended up with the patients his colleague found uninteresting. He soon became disillusioned and the two doctors fell out with each other. One bust-up too many ended with Doyle ripping the name-plate from his door and storming out. He left to set up his own surgery at Southsea, choosing the city of Portsmouth because of its resemblance to Plymouth. Doyle's experiences at Dr Budd's surgery were reflected in The Stark Munro Letters.

Novelist DANIEL DEFOE - author of Robinson Crusoe - fell in love with the view from Plymouth Hoe. He came to Plymouth on his famous Tour Through the Whole Island of Great Britain. Looking out to Plymouth Sound on a summer evening, he said he had never seen a sight so serene. Ironically, the following night, Defoe witnessed a terrific storm from the Hoe. His peaceful Plymouth Sound the following morning was littered with nothing, but the remains of wrecked ships.

One of the most striking features of Plymouth is the previously mentioned remains of Charles Church which sit on a roundabout at Charles Cross. A former vicar of the church was the grandfather of poet R.S. HAWKER - the famous vicar of Morwenstow. Robert Stephen Hawker was born at Charles Church Vicarage in 1803. He was baptised at Stoke Damerel where his father was curate. Hawker will be remembered for The Song of the Western Men and his eccentric ways. Contrary to his wishes to be buried at his beloved Morwenstow on the north Cornish coast, Hawker was laid to rest in his home city after his death in 1875. Controversial to the last, he converted to Catholicism on his death bed, as his tombstone in Plymouth's Ford Park Cemetery testifies. The simple granite cross can be found at the northern end of the cemetery. Hawker's second wife was buried beside him.

The visitor can leave the hustle and bustle of the city centre and step back in time via Plymouth Barbican. The Barbican, with its narrow quayside alleyways, has remained unchanged for centuries, escaping Hitler's bombs. It is situated east of Plymouth Hoe and encapsulates Sutton Harbour. The harbour probably has more stories to tell than any other place in England! It was from here the Pilgrim Fathers and other adventurers such as Drake, Raleigh, Hawkins and Cook left in search of better things.

It is easy to believe you are back in Elizabethan England, and at any minute, Drake and Co. will come sailing into the harbour. Novelist NICHOLAS MONSARRAT - best-known for The Cruel Sea - shared the same thoughts when he penned part of The Master Mariner at Plymouth. Monsarrat gives an insight into Plymouth life just before the Armada confrontation. He describes the city and its people through the eyes of Francis Drake's coxswain, Matthew Lawe. The three-volume novel focused on seafaring life from Napoleonic times to the present. The author died before completing the second volume.

Plymouth has had many natives who have gone on to great things in the literary world. WILLIAM CROSSING was born here, as was HENRY AUSTIN DOBSON - the poet and author of the famous Eighteenth Century Vignettes. He was born at Park Street in 1840. The house no longer exists.

J.C. SQUIRE, another native, attended the city's former Grammar School, which was also situated at Park Street. He became a successful poet and critic, and founded the London Mercury in 1919. He was a strong literary figure who did much to spread the knowledge of American Literature in England.

L.A.G. STRONG was another who spent his childhood in the city. He lived at Mutley Park House in Oxford Avenue. He recalls the house and city in his novel, The Garden. It was writing about Dartmoor which changed his fortunes, however. His successful 1929 Dartmoor novel, Dewer Rides, allowed him to give up teaching and become a full-time writer.

Another interesting character born at Plymouth was novelist MORTIMER COLLINS - alias The King of the Bohemians. His work included The Vivian Romance and The Secret of Long Life. The latter was written in 1871. Interestingly, Collins died of heart disease five years later - at the ripe old age of 49!

Saltram House, a mile east of Plymouth just off the A38, is well worth a visit. Diarist FANNY BURNEY fell in love with the magnificent Georgian building on her visit to the area and described it fondly in her diaries. Dr Samuel Johnson also came here on occasions with local painter Joshua Reynolds. The house, now owned by the National Trust, contains many fine portraits by Reynolds. The house is open to the public during the summer.

Where the South Devon Coast Path begins at Turnchapel, on the eastern side of Plymouth, is another interesting literary connection.

T.E. LAWRENCE - better known as Lawrence of Arabia - spent a spell here at Mount Batten in the Flying Boat Squadron under the name of Aircraftman Shaw. A commemorative plaque can be found on the wall of the corner house at St John's Road, close to the entrance to Mount Batten. Lawrence was both a fine soldier and a fine writer. His greatest literary work was The Seven Pillars of Wisdom, though he also published an accessible translation of Homer's Ancient Greek classic, The Odyssey, in 1932. Lawrence was often seen whizzing around the South Devon lanes on his motorcycle. It was a motorcycle crash in Dorset which killed him in 1935.

SARAH MARTIN

The name will be unfamiliar to most - but the work of Sarah Martin is familiar in almost every household in Britain. She was the author of the classic nursery rhyme, Old Mother Hubbard, a story conceived on the outskirts of Plymouth.

Places to see: Yealmpton: Old Mother Hubbard's Cottage.

Old Mother Hubbard's Cottage sits on the main A379 coast road in the village of Yealmpton, seven miles from Plymouth.
The star of the popular rhyme was an old housekeeper who lived at the cottage while she looked after a house called Kitley - about a mile away. Sarah Martin, also occasionally referred to as Sarah Oliver, came to live at the house for a period when her sister married the squire and owner of Kitley. The library at Kitley contains the only-known copy of the first edition of the Mother Hubbard rhyme which Sarah Martin wrote in 1805.

Old Mother Hubbard's Cottage at Yealmpton.

The poem's 28 verses formed a comprehensive list of local shops and pubs. The reference to the cupboard being bare was because of a shortage of food due to the Napoleonic Wars. The cottage is now a restaurant, but still one of the most-photographed buildings in Devon. Kitley House is not visible from the road and not open to the public.

The South Devon coast, with its delightful estuaries and secluded coves, has attracted numerous visitors. Our tour along its shores begins at the resort of Bigbury-on-Sea, which is well worth a visit for two literary connections. Burgh Island, which sits opposite the main beach, is where AGATHA CHRISTIE set at least one of her novels. The island became Smuggler's Island in Evil Under the Sun and may have also partly-inspired her classic Ten Little Niggers, later renamed And Then There Were None. In the book, ten people - all with guilty secrets - are lured to the island and killed off one by one. Many say Burgh Island is nothing like the island in the book - Burgh Island is far closer to the shore than Nigger Island - but it certainly may have triggered off some thoughts in the author's head.

Visitors to Burgh Island will also find it difficult to become stranded. The island is easily reached by low tide or via the resort's unique sea tractor during high tide. Unlike the poor victims of the book, many choose to stay at the island and book a room at its lovely hotel. The hotel is decorated and furnished in the style of the 1920s. A stay here will really help the Christie fan return to the era she became famous.

An inland walk of about one-and-a-half miles to the picturesque village of Ringmore is enjoyed by many visitors to Bigbury Bay. Their journey's end is often, quite literally, the Journey's End! This is a pub which was named after the World War One play by R.C. SHERRIFF. He wrote the successful play while lodging at the inn. It is the perfect place to rest your weary feet. Sherriff was also a successful screen-writer. His film credits include The Invisible Man, Goodbye Mr Chips, Odd Man Out and The Dam Busters.

Further along the coast is the busy fishing town of Salcombe - Devon's sailing mecca. This is certainly the place to come if you like watching boats. LORD ALFRED TENNYSON did just that. He came in the summer of 1889 and was inspired to pen Crossing the Bar after watching boats attempt to navigate the difficult passage into the harbour. The actual poem was written some time later on the Isle of White.

Tennyson stayed at the home of historian J.A. FROUDE. Froude spent many summers at The Moult before retiring to Salcombe for good and taking up residence at Woodville, now known as Woodcot. Both houses are situated in extensive grounds on the road to Bolt Head between North and South Sands.

Beautiful Burgh Island inspired Agatha Christie.

Sadly, Froude, who was born at Dartington, near Totnes, died soon after moving to Salcombe. He was buried in the town's cemetery.

At the head of the estuary is the market town of Kingsbridge and another literary connection. This was the home town of John Wolcot, alias satirist PETER PINDAR. He was born at Pindar Lodge in the parish of Dodbrooke in 1738 and went on to be educated at Kingsbridge Free School. Pindar Lodge can be found on The Quay, a stone's throw from the head of the estuary. It is now a private residence and not open to the public. Pindar spent most of his life in London where he became one of the country's leading satirists. King George III was a target of his wit. Pindar is best-remembered as the author of the satirical Lyric Odes to the Royal Academicians.

Poet and novelist JOHN MASEFIELD visited Salcombe and Kingsbridge while living at the heart of the Gara Valley. The valley, which sits in the beautiful South Hams, is a fine place to escape from the hustle and bustle of life. Masefield was a close friend of Irish artist Jack Yeats and was invited to stay at his cottage at the beginning of the century. He joined the brother of poet W.B. Yeats in the spring of 1903. The cottage was called Snail's Castle, as it was situated on the eastern side of the valley, which was home to a large population of snails. The two men enjoyed many boyish activities together, such as making and sailing model boats on the Gara trout stream which runs through the valley. Masefield enjoyed long walks around the Slapton area which was to feature in many poems and novels.

His 1911 children's novel Jim Davis - a smuggling tale - was set in the Gara Valley. Snail's Castle and the Gara stream feature, as does Blackpool Sands, near Dartmouth, where the author set the caves frequented by the smugglers. The book's two main characters are based on Masefield and Yeats. The maritime town of Dartmouth has a few literary connections itself.

GEOFFREY CHAUCER based his Shipman from The Canterbury Tales on local tycoon John Hawley. The 14th-century author could not fail to notice Hawley when he visited the port in 1373, for the rich merchant was chief shipowner and the town's most-influential figure at the time. St Saviour's Church has a brass of Hawley within its walls. Chaucer - working as a customs officer - was sent to Dartmouth by Edward III to investigate the seizure of a ship belonging to a merchant from Genoa. The King wished to remain on good terms with the merchant, so Chaucer, having just returned from Italy and a speaker of the language, was judged the best person to deal with the delicate situation.

Beautiful Dartmouth also became the home of novelist FLORA THOMPSON from 1928 to 1940. Flora was known as the country girl whose life story became a classic. Her trilogy, Lark Rise to Candleford, set in North Oxfordshire where she spent most of her life, was actually written in Devon. The family moved to the county when her husband John became postmaster of Dartmouth. They lived at a cottage called The Outlook - 126 Above Town - which overlooked the Dart Estuary. It was here Flora began working on Lark Rise which was published in 1939 when the author was 62-years-old. John retired in 1940 and the family moved the short distance to Brixham. Flora died in 1947. Her grave is tucked away in the corner of Longcross Cemetery on the outskirts of Dartmouth. The headstone is shaped in the form of an open book and has her name on one page and the name of her beloved son, Peter, who lost his life during the war, on the other.

Dartmouth was frequently visited by AGATHA CHRISTIE while she lived further up the Dart at Greenway. The town featured as itself in Ordeal by Innocence and was also the setting for the short-story, The Regatta Mystery. The visitor may like to continue to the head of the estuary and to Totnes, which was once home to Irish playwright SEAN O'CASEY. He moved to the town in 1938 so his children could attend Dartington Hall School. The family home was Tingrith on the Ashburton Road. They stayed here for 17 years before moving to Torquay.

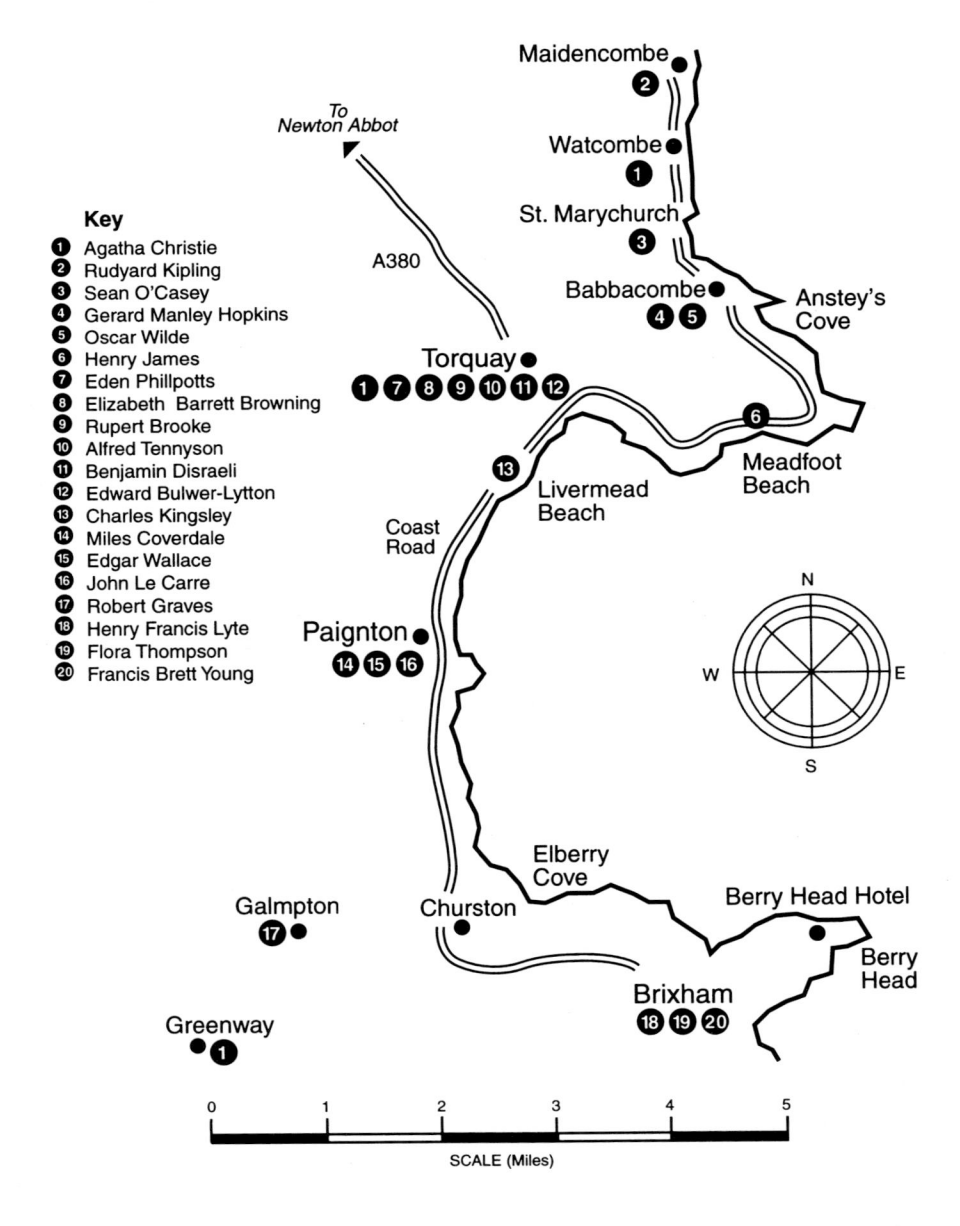

TORBAY

TORBAY

Key
1. Agatha Christie
2. Rudyard Kipling
3. Sean O'Casey
4. Gerard Manley Hopkins
5. Oscar Wilde
6. Henry James
7. Eden Phillpotts
8. Elizabeth Barrett Browning
9. Rupert Brooke
10. Alfred Tennyson
11. Benjamin Disraeli
12. Edward Bulwer-Lytton
13. Charles Kingsley
14. Miles Coverdale
15. Edgar Wallace
16. John Le Carre
17. Robert Graves
18. Henry Francis Lyte
19. Flora Thompson
20. Francis Brett Young

The English Riviera - a pseudonym for Torbay - has never had any problem attracting visitors. It was once extremely fashionable to be seen in the area and so regularly frequented by the rich and famous, many of whom were men and women of letters.

Torquay - often referred to as the jewel in the Torbay crown - has played host to most literary visitors to the area, though Paignton and Brixham can also claim a share. The latter became the final home of Henry Francis Lyte - one of the country's finest hymn-writers.

Not every famous writer came from outside the county, however. One of the world's most-popular authors was born in Torquay itself. Agatha Christie is arguably Devon's most-successful writer and responsible for bringing even more visitors to this already-busy corner of the county.

AGATHA CHRISTIE

Agatha Christie is often regarded as the world's most-popular author.

Worldwide, she has only been out-sold by William Shakespeare and The Bible. Her classic whodunnits have been translated into more than 40 different languages.

The work of Agatha Christie has been adapted for almost every medium. The Mousetrap - based on her short-story Three Blind Mice - is still the world's longest running stage play and set to keep on running.

As well as her crime novels, Agatha Christie wrote poetry and romantic novels under the pseudonym Mary Westmacott, but it was her 66 whodunnit novels and numerous short-stories with which she will be remembered. Her famous detectives, Hercule Poirot and Miss Marple, have become household names and helped make the South Devon author the undisputed Queen of Crime.

Places to see: Torquay: coast path walk - Imperial Hotel - memorial bust - Torquay Museum - Town Hall - Torre Abbey - Grand Hotel.
Churston: Churston Church. Galmpton: Greenway House.

Nobody could have imagined the impact Agatha Christie would have on the world of fiction when she took up an informal challenge to write a detective book. The gauntlet had been thrown down by her eldest sister at the family home of Ashfield at Barton, Torquay. The book became The Mysterious Affair at Styles and was the beginning of a remarkable career which made Agatha Christie one of the most-popular authors in the world.

Unfortunately, Ashfield - the house where Agatha was born in 1890 - no longer exists. Barton Road, where it stood, is still worth a visit just to see how much the area has changed since Agatha's day. In fact, it was changing fast even while she was alive. The house was actually demolished in 1961 to make way for an extension to South Devon College. Agatha, who had left it long ago, actually tried to buy it back in the hope of turning it into an old people's home. The house - one of her earliest memories - features in her final book, Postern of Fate. The garden of the book had a greenhouse containing a rocking horse which was believed to be identical to the one at Ashfield.

The best place to begin a tour of Agatha Christie's Torbay is on the coast path at Torquay Golf Course, which is found on the Torquay to Teignmouth road at Watcombe. A plateau on the cliff-edge below the course is believed to be the scene of the crime in Why Didn't They Ask Evans. Agatha loved the sea and regularly walked this stretch of coast. The path passes a number of secluded beaches before dropping to popular Oddicombe and Babbacombe beaches. The family regularly came here to bathe.

After admiring the wonderful view from Walls Hill, the walker is taken down a steep flight of steps to Redgate Beach and Anstey's Cove. Agatha loved this secluded spot and would enjoy moonlit picnics here.

The coast path stretches approximately three miles before passing Beacon Cove and dropping to Torquay Harbour. At the end of the path is the impressive five-star Imperial Hotel. This featured in a number of Agatha's novels. Miss Marple delivers her postscript in Sleeping Murder

Agatha Christie takes pride of place at the centre of Torquay.

while sitting on the terrace of the hotel. The hotel also appeared in Peril at End House and The Body in the Library under the name, The Majestic Hotel. The End House in the former was based on Rock End, a small cliff-top house which once stood close to the Imperial.

Beacon Cove was another favourite bathing spot - being the ladies' bathing beach of the day.

A memorial to Agatha Christie can be found in the form of a commemorative bust close to the harbour in front of the Pavilion Shopping Centre. This was once a theatre and regularly frequented by Agatha and her family, who were great fans of the stage.

Two places slightly inland which are worth a visit are Kent's Cavern and Torquay Museum. The prehistoric Kent's Cavern, found at Wellswood, was featured in The Man in the Brown Suit under the name Hampsly Cavern. The museum houses an Agatha Christie exhibition which no Christie fan can afford to miss!

Torquay Town Hall sits about a mile from the harbour in the centre of the town at Castle Circus. It is reached through the many high street shops. It was here Agatha worked during the First World War as a Red Cross nurse in a temporary war hospital, which had been set up within these walls. Her vast knowledge of poisons was gained during a spell at a dispensary shortly afterwards. Of her 66 novels - 41 of them involved poison in some way. It is hardly surprising The Mysterious Affair at Styles was one of them. Agatha began the book while working at the town hall. It is incredible to think the novel was initially rejected by a number of publishers before being published in 1920.

Memories of her time at the dispensary surfaced some 50 years later. Agatha never forgot her boss, Torquay's best-known pharmacist, and used him as a character in The Pale Horse. He once showed her a dark-coloured substance and told her it was curare. He informed her it was fatal and at the same time added the fact he kept it in his pocket because it made him feel powerful!

Another place worth a visit is Torre Abbey, which sits facing the sea on the main Torbay road. The building - which is open to the public - contains an Agatha Christie Memorial Room. Within view of Torre Abbey, sitting beside Torquay Station, is the Grand Hotel. This is where Agatha spent a brief honeymoon with her first husband, Archibald Christie, before being temporarily separated due to the First World War. Corbyn Head, a grassy mound sitting opposite, became Baldy's Head in Postern of Fate .

Torquay featured in a number of Agatha's novels, usually disguised under a different name. It became St Loo in Peril at End House; Loomouth in Three

Act Tragedy; Danemouth in The Body in the Library and Cullenquay in Mrs McGinty's Dead. Hercule Poirot was also conceived in the town. He was based on one of the Belgian refugees living at Torquay during the war.

Paignton and Brixham have fewer obvious connections with Agatha Christie. One place well worth a visit, however, is the village of Churston, which is situated about a mile from Brixham. The church has a stained glass window donated by Agatha, while nearby Elberry Cove was the scene of the third grisly crime in The ABC Murders.

Inland and two miles from Churston Station is Greenway - hidden away on the banks of the River Dart at Galmpton. Greenway - once the home of Humphrey Gilbert, half-cousin of Walter Raleigh - became the family home after Ashfield was sold in 1938. Greenway appeared as Alderbury in Five Little Pigs and as Nasse House in Dead Man's Folly. The murder in the latter book was set in the boathouse at Greenway.

The Georgian house is still owned by the Christie family and so is not open to the public. The best way to view it is from the River Dart itself. Regular boat trips operate from Dartmouth and Totnes.

There were many other writers who were influenced by this part of the county.

Our literary tour of Torbay, which can be combined with the above Agatha Christie tour, begins on the outskirts of Torquay at the coastal village of Maidencombe.

Just off the main coast road is Rockhouse Lane. Novelist RUDYARD KIPLING and his wife moved to Rock House at the top of the road in September 1896. Kipling described the house as a dream home, but his time here was a generally unhappy one, as he was suffering from depression. He did manage to pen some of his finest work at Rock House, however. He wrote The Day's Work and also began Stalky & Co while living in the village. Rock House was also featured in The House Surgeon.

Irish-born playwright SEAN O'CASEY once lived at Villa Rosa in Trumlands Road, St Marychurch. He arrived from Totnes, moving to a flat in the large Victorian house, now number 40. O'Casey stayed at Villa Rosa until his death in 1964. He is best-remembered for his strong political views. His 1926 play, The Plough and the Stars, provoked a full-scale riot in his home country. Other Irish-based plays such as The Bishop's Bonfire and The Drums of Father Ned were written in Devon.

Further along the coastal road, situated on the north coast of Torquay, is Babbacombe. GERARD MANLEY HOPKINS was inspired by the view from Babbacombe Downs and it is easy to see why. On a clear day the view extends all the way along the South Devon coast into Dorset. He saved some of his most-beautiful lines for lovely Babbacombe Bay.

Another visitor to Babbacombe was the controversial genius OSCAR WILDE. He came at the height of his fame and lodged at Babbacombe Cliff - the home of Lady Georgina Mount Temple. Lady Mount Temple - her statue can be found at Babbacombe Downs - was a popular figure in her time and a distant relative of Mrs Wilde. She leased the house, now a hotel, to the Wilde family for three months in the early 1890s. Wilde completed A Woman of No Importance during his time here and also attended rehearsals for his play, Lady Windermere's Fan, which opened in January 1893 at the Royal Theatre in Abbey Road. The theatre - found at the centre of Torquay - was converted to a cinema in 1933.

One of the finest walks Torquay has to offer is along the coast path from Babbacombe to Torquay Harbour. On the way - a mere mile from the harbour - is Meadfoot Beach and the crescent-shaped Osborne Hotel. Novelist and short-story writer HENRY JAMES often stayed here and began writing The Spoils of Poynton during one stay in 1895.

James also paid visits to the childhood home of Agatha Christie at Barton Road, being a friend of the family. Agatha was too young to remember much of James, but she did recall the strange way he took his tea. The American, who was himself famous for writing about the eccentric ways of the English upper-class, always asked for one lump of sugar to be broken into two! James is remembered for his detailed works, such as The Ambassadors, and for the classic ghost story, The Turn of the Screw.

Novelist EDEN PHILLPOTTS was another who regularly dropped in at the home of young Agatha. The Dartmoor author was a neighbour, living at Eltham in Oakhill Road. He moved to Eltham in 1901 and wrote most of his novels there. Agatha frequently came to him for advice. Thomas Hardy, Arnold Bennett and J.K. Jerome were also visitors to his home.

Torquay Harbour was the pleasant view short-story writer ELIZABETH BARRETT BROWNING was faced with during her spell at Torquay. She came in 1838 in the hope the mild climate would improve her health. She lived at Bath House in Beacon Terrace, now replaced by the Regina Hotel. A plaque records the fact she stayed for about three years. Elizabeth actually hated most of her time at Torquay and described it as a place which did her more harm than good. Her feelings were not helped by the tragic death of her favourite brother, who died during a sailing accident at Babbacombe Bay in 1840. The writer was grief-stricken and went into a psychic state of shock. Already a tiny, frail woman, and a semi-invalid after a pony accident at the age of 15, she retreated into a shell and spent most of her time like a locked-up prisoner. It was her marriage to Robert Browning and a move back to the capital which eventually freed her.

Somebody who did enjoy his stay at Torquay was poet RUPERT BROOKE. He so liked the resort after a visit in 1908, he is believed to have based his famous sonnet, Seaside, here.

LORD ALFRED TENNYSON is another who could not resist the charms of Torquay and described it as being 'the loveliest sea-village in England'. He stayed in the resort in 1838 and had a particular soft spot for Torre Abbey, which sits facing the beach. Audley Court is believed to have been based on the famous abbey.

Perhaps Torquay's most-distinguished resident was prime minister BENJAMIN DISRAELI. The politician and novelist spent many summers at fashionable Torquay, lodging at the former Royal Hotel when he visited in the mid-1850s. Disraeli, who later took the title Earl of Beaconsfield, often visited close friend Sarah Brydges Willyams and inherited her Mount Braddon home after her death. He is believed to have got the idea for The Primrose League when he spotted a bowl of primroses during one of her dinner parties. The statesman wrote a number of novels, including Vivian Grey and the trilogy consisting of Coningsby, Sybil and Tancred. His literary work was not surprisingly overshadowed by his political life, however. Disraeli was twice prime minister before his death in 1881.

Versatile writer EDWARD BULWER-LYTTON also bought a home at mild Torquay to spend the long, cold winter months. He first came to the resort in 1856 and liked it so much, kept returning, eventually buying Argyll Hall in Warren Road. Disraeli was a regular visitor and Charles Dickens was a life-long friend. It is believed Bulwer-Lytton persuaded the novelist to change the end of Great Expectations.

Bulwer-Lytton wrote numerous novels himself, his most-famous being The Last Days of Pompeii and Rienzi. He was also one of the most-successful playwrights of his time. His plays held the stage for long periods, even after his death. Bulwer-Lytton died in 1873 after catching a chill at his hill-top Warren Road home. The walk up to Warren Road - now a haven for hotels - is well worth the effort for the magnificent views it boasts. The best way to reach it is via the entwining paths belonging to Rock Walk. The prominent cliff-face is illuminated by coloured lights after dark.

On the outskirts of Torquay, on the road to Paignton, is Livermead Beach and the prominent Livermead Hotel. North Devon novelist CHARLES KINGSLEY lived at a cottage here for a brief spell in the mid-19th century.

The family home was Livermead Cottage, which sat at the entrance to Livermead Beach. They had come in the hope the mild climate would improve the health of Mrs Kingsley. The family did not stay long, however, packing their bags when the Bishop of Exeter banned Kingsley from all the town's pulpits because of the Socialist material found in his early works.

The resort of Paignton sits at the centre of the bay - about three miles from Torquay. It has fewer literary connections to Torquay and its grandest literary claim to fame may not even be justified. The claim is that 16th-century Bible translator MILES COVERDALE visited the town.

Tourists can visit Coverdale Tower - found in the old part of Paignton just off the main street - which formed part of the old palace belonging to the Bishops of Exeter. It is claimed Coverdale - who is credited with the translation of the first complete English text of The Bible - lodged here to work on the translation. There has been much debate on the subject in recent years, with some now claiming he did not even set foot in the town. Paigntonians will tell you different, however!

Another literary figure who is said to have resided for a spell at Paignton is thriller writer EDGAR WALLACE. He stayed in the resort on a number of occasions during the latter stages of his life. It is believed he resided at Grosvenor House, now a residential home, at the junction of Grosvenor Road and Fisher Street. Wallace was a patron of the local cinema, which still stands next to the railway station at the centre of Paignton. He was a prolific writer of detective books and once dictated a complete novel in one weekend.

Fellow-thriller writer JOHN LE CARRE is believed to have used Paignton for the opening of A Perfect Spy. A number of South Devon coastal resorts claim the statistic, though the description of spy Magnus Pym alighting from his taxi to 'disappear' to write his memoirs, best fits Paignton.

Between Paignton and Brixham, set back from the coast, is the village of Galmpton. Poet and novelist ROBERT GRAVES lived here for six years during World War Two. Villagers were at first suspicious of Graves. The local policeman discovered his middle name was von Ranke and believed he might have German sympathies. The family soon settled in, however, and described Galmpton as a lovely place to live. Three of the author's children were born while Graves and Beryl Hodge, who eventually became his second wife, resided at Vale House Farm. Graves will be remembered for his controversial memoirs, Goodbye To All That, and the 1934 novel I, Claudius.

HENRY FRANCIS LYTE

Sitting at the far side of Torbay is Brixham. The charming fishing town became home to one of the country's greatest hymn-writers. The Rev Henry Francis Lyte is best-remembered for the popular hymn, Abide With Me.

Places to see: Brixham: All Saints' Church - Berry Head House.

Visitors to Brixham will not fail to spot the church where Henry Francis Lyte served for 23 years. All Saints' Church rises high above the town and is one of the bay's most-prominent landmarks. Lyte came to Brixham in 1824 and originally began preaching at St Mary's Church, before becoming the first vicar of All Saints' Church. He held the post until his untimely death in 1847 at the age of 54.

All Saints' Church towers above busy Brixham Harbour.

The church is a fine place to begin a short literary tour of Lyte's Brixham. Inside, in the silence, you can still sense his presence. It is easy to take yourself back 150 years or so and imagine being among his congregation. The local fishing community - which made up most of the flock - loved Lyte and he loved them. The harbour is a stone's throw from here. Lyte would bless the fishermen as they went off to sea. He would never let a new ship set sail without first having blessed it. Every skipper was presented with a copy of The Bible.

The Lytes first lived in a dreary house at Burton Street before moving to a superb cliff-side home beneath Berry Head. Berry Head House, now a hotel, is reached via a mile-walk from the harbour towards Berry Head Country Park. A plaque can be found on the wall of the building. Lyte loved his home and its fine views of Torbay. He built up an extensive library here, which became the envy of many West Country historians. It is inside where he also

Berry Head House was where Brixham hymn-writer Henry Francis Lyte wrote Abide with Me.

wrote his hymns and poems, the latter were based on many of his congregation. Despite his popularity, Lyte was not content with his writing and, knowing he was dying, prayed for the inspiration to compose one more song which would be of lasting benefit to mankind. Abide With Me was the answer to the Brixham vicar's prayers - believed to be written at his Berry Head home just a few weeks before his death. There are some who say the world-famous hymn was actually written on the afternoon of the day of his final sermon.
Lyte left Brixham a few weeks later bound for the continent in a bid to improve his fading health. A large crowd of parishioners and fishermen lined the streets to wave goodbye. They must have known in their hearts he would not be coming back. He died in Nice a few weeks later and was laid to rest in the French city.
Those who gathered for the memorial service at Brixham paid the greatest respect to their beloved vicar by singing the hymn he wanted to be remembered for.
Brixham also became the final home of novelist FLORA THOMPSON. She

moved here in 1940 when her husband retired from his job at Dartmouth. They settled at Lauriston, an old cottage hidden away from the sea and town centre in Higher Brixham. The cottage, which can be found at New Road, closely resembled a house described in her unfinished novel Dashpers, which was written in the town. Flora later bought another house at Bolton Street as an investment. Still Glides the Stream - her final book - was finished just weeks before her death in 1947. She died of heart failure alone in her room. She was buried at Dartmouth.

Physician and author FRANCIS BRETT YOUNG set up his first medical practice at Brixham. He arrived in 1907 and stayed until the outbreak of the First World War, living at Cleveland House. It was here he took up writing his first novel, Deep Sea, which was set in the town and published in 1914. Young is best-known for his post-war novels, set in his native Midlands, which include the hugely-successful, My Brother Jonathan.

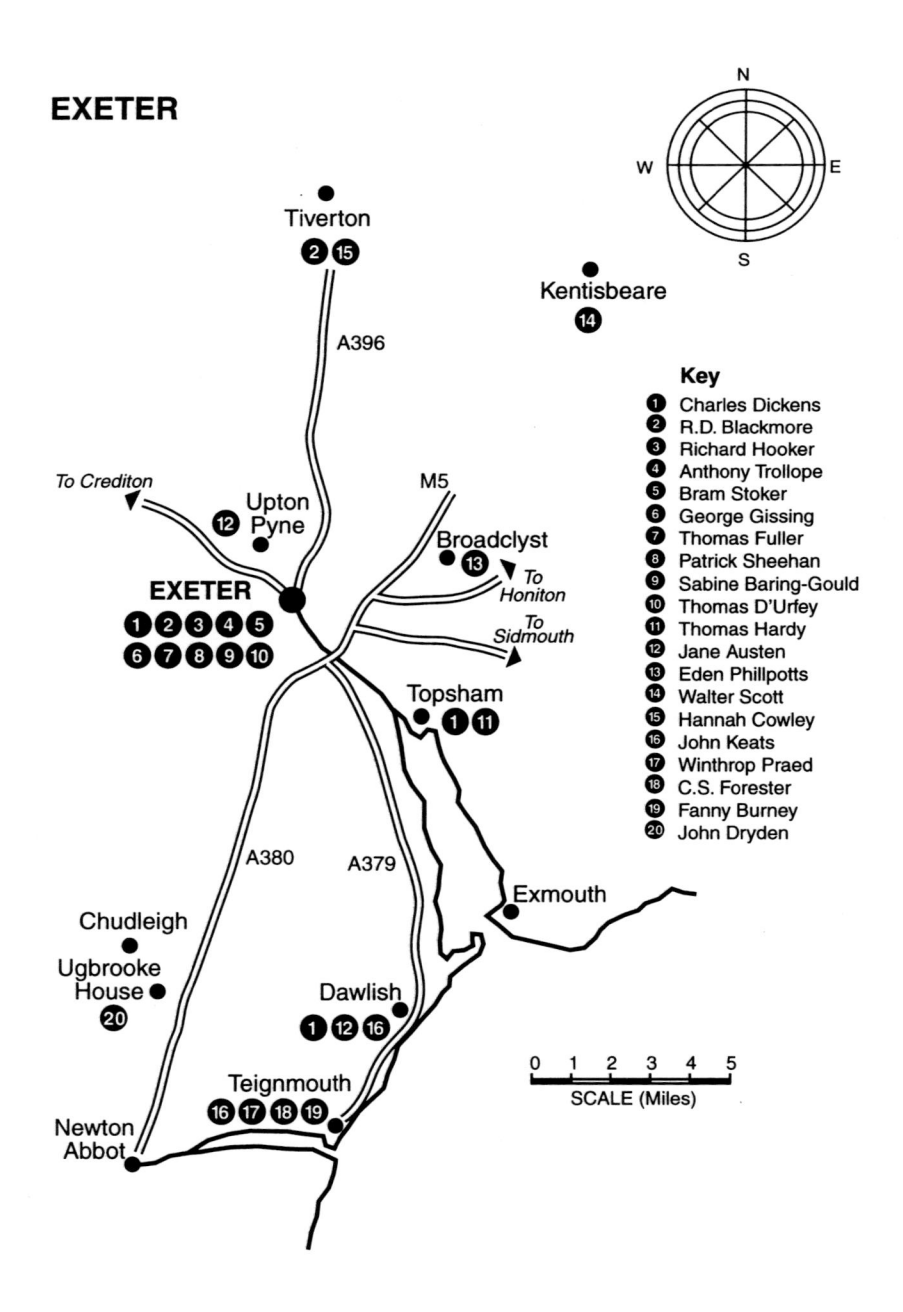

EXETER

EXETER

Key
1. Charles Dickens
2. R.D. Blackmore
3. Richard Hooker
4. Anthony Trollope
5. Bram Stoker
6. George Gissing
7. Thomas Fuller
8. Patrick Sheehan
9. Sabine Baring-Gould
10. Thomas D'Urfey
11. Thomas Hardy
12. Jane Austen
13. Eden Phillpotts
14. Walter Scott
15. Hannah Cowley
16. John Keats
17. Winthrop Praed
18. C.S. Forester
19. Fanny Burney
20. John Dryden

The county town of Devon and its surrounding area is not surprisingly home to a number of literary connections.

Charles Dickens is the most-famous author to revel in the delights of the city. The nearby resort of Teignmouth had poet John Keats as a resident for a brief period, while Jane Austen fell in love with a rural village north of Exeter.

CHARLES DICKENS

Charles Dickens was one of the greatest writers the country has ever produced. His novels - many of which were published in serial form - had the nation gripped from start to finish. Devon played quite an important part in the life of the young author and many of its inhabitants became the inspiration for some of his most-famous characters.

Places to see: Alphington: Mile End Cottage.
Exeter: Turk's Head - Rougemont Castle.

Alphington sits on the outskirts of Exeter. Here you will find the most-permanent reminder of the author's connection with the county.
Mile End Cottage - on busy Church Road - became home to his parents for four years from 1839. Charles rented the cottage on their behalf in a bid to keep them out of trouble! His father, who was imprisoned for debt when Charles was a child, had again got himself into financial difficulties. Dickens junior decided there would be fewer temptations in the countryside away from London. He knew Exeter well and, believing the area to be 'the most beautiful in this most beautiful of English counties,' thought it best-suited to his parents.
Exeter, though it is difficult to believe looking at it these days, had not been swamped by concrete buildings and Mile End Cottage, with its delightful thatched roof, stood isolated. How things have changed!
Charles paid the rent and for all the necessary furnishings the cottage needed. He may have had an ulterior motive for sending his parents packing from the capital, however, for many believe the aspiring novelist found them a social embarrassment! His parents and their young son, Augustus, were at first content with country living, but they slowly began to crave for London. Charles finally relented and allowed them to move back to the capital four years later.
Charles regularly visited his parents at Alphington. The opening chapters of Nicholas Nickleby were written at Mile End Cottage. The character of Mrs Nickleby was based on his own mother, while Mrs Lupin of

the Blue Dragon in Martin Chuzzlewit, was inspired by the landlady at Mile End. His feckless father, John, later became the inspiration for Mr Micawber in David Copperfield. The cottage, now a private residence, has a plaque on its wall.

The one-and-a-half mile walk from the cottage to the city centre today is hardly as pleasant as when Dickens would have made it, but well worth the

Mile End Cottage has changed a lot since Charles Dickens rented it for his parents.

effort. A fine spot to rest your weary feet and find refreshment is the 15th-century Turk's Head, which is situated in the busy high street. It was here Dickens spotted a rather overweight boot boy, who was to become The Fat Boy in his first novel, The Pickwick Papers. The pub became a regular port of call whenever the author was in town.

Dickens first came to the city in 1835 as a parliamentary reporter for the Morning Chronicle. The young journalist stood in the pouring rain in the yard at Rougemont Castle to report on a pre-election speech by MP Lord John Russell. He raced back to London by coach, transcribing his shorthand on the way and bribing the post boys en route, to ensure his paper printed the story ahead of The Times.

Dickens once lodged at the New London Inn - now an office block - while giving two public readings in the city. He described the Exeter audience as the finest he had ever read to.

It is not really known how far Dickens ventured from Exeter during his many visits. He is known to have based the sly Pecksniff from Martin Chuzzlewit on a Topsham resident, and used Dawlish as the literary birthplace of Nicholas in Nicholas Nickleby. Nicholas is born at a farm on the outskirts of the town. The farm is sold, but Nicholas buys it at the end of the novel when he finally prospers. Both resorts, lying either side of the Exe Estuary, are well worth a visit.

The city of Exeter has been home to a number of writers. Our literary tour of the city, which can be combined with a tour of Dickens' Exeter, begins inside the magnificent Exeter Cathedral.

Just inside the building is a plaque dedicated to novelist R.D. BLACKMORE. It was unveiled by Dartmoor novelist Eden Phillpotts.

Outside the cathedral is a fine statue of theologian RICHARD HOOKER - one of Exeter's most-treasured sons. Hooker was born in the Heavitree area of the city and educated here in the mid-16th century. He became labelled as the greatest apologist of the Anglican church. His famous, Of the Laws of Ecclesiastical Polity, was an apology for the Elizabethan religious and political settlement.

Dickens was a regular visitor to the Turk's Head and conceived one of his earliest characters here.

Cathedral Close, with its famous Mol's Coffee House, is found opposite Hooker's statue. To the east of the 16th-century black-and-white building, now a jewellers, are a row of elegant houses. Novelist ANTHONY TROLLOPE, best-known for his Barchester Chronicles, often came here to visit his mother's friend, Fanny Bird, who lived in one of the houses. He used Mrs Bird as the model for Miss Jemima Stanbury in He Knew He Was Right.

Miss Stanbury claims: 'In Exeter the only place for a lady was the Close'. Visitors to this impressive part of the city will no doubt agree. BRAM STOKER also chose Cathedral Close as the place from which Jonathan Harker leaves for Transylvania in the classic Dracula.

Exeter became the home and inspiration for novelist GEORGE GISSING for two years in the late 19th century. He arrived from London in 1891 and was soon to appreciate the peace and tranquillity compared to the hustle and bustle of life in the capital. He wrote to say how relieved he was to wake every morning to silence! He is known to have lodged at two properties during his stay - 24 Prospect Park, just off Old Tiverton Road, and 1 St Leonard's Terrace, just off Topsham Road. Born in Exile and The Private Papers of Henry Ryecroft both feature the city and its surrounding area.

Theologian Richard Hooker proudly sits within the shadow of Exeter Cathedral.

Another literary figure to come to Exeter was theologian THOMAS FULLER. He came with the Royalists in 1643 and preached in the city in between working on The History of the Worthies of England, a countrywide survey which was published in 1662, a year after his death. Fuller spent most of his life as a royal chaplain, but was later believed to be one of the first writers in England to earn a living by his pen.

Another member of the clergy to enjoy a brief stay at Exeter was Irish novelist and priest PATRICK SHEEHAN. He came to the city shortly after being ordained in 1875 and stayed for two years, before returning to Ireland, the setting for his novels.

Home-bred authors include hymn-writer SABINE BARING-GOULD. He was born in the city in 1834. The popular vicar moved to West Devon and made his name with the famous hymn, Onward, Christian Soldiers.

Poet and dramatist THOMAS D'URFEY was born at Exeter in 1653. He made his name in London, writing powerful melodramas and boisterous farces. His most-famous work was the 1719 Wit and Mirth, or Pills to Purge Melancholy.

THOMAS HARDY used Exeter in four of his novels. The city appeared as Exonbury in The Trumpet-Major, The Woodlanders, Jude the Obscure and A Pair of Blue Eyes.

Nearby Topsham was also visited by Hardy. He came to the town in 1890 after the death of close friend Tryphena Sparks. He cycled from his Dorchester home to place flowers on her grave. Her daughter Nellie became the inspiration for the poem To a Motherless Child.

JANE AUSTEN

Jane Austen is regarded as one of the greats of English Literature.

She wrote about the middle-class society she knew so well. Her six great novels - which mainly centred on the quest of young women to find suitable husbands - continue to grow in reputation as the years go by. The most-famous and widely read is Pride and Prejudice.

Places to see: Upton Pyne: Church of Our Lady - Woodrow Barton - Pynes.

Fond memories of a holiday in the Exeter area persuaded Jane Austen to set her first novel in the region. The area in question was the pretty village of Upton Pyne, which is found just off the busy A377 road four miles from the centre of Exeter. Jane stayed in the village with friends at the beginning of the 19th century. It left a lasting impression on her as she used it for the setting of Barton Valley in her first novel, Sense and Sensibility, which was published in 1811.

The best place to start a short walk to the places associated with Jane Austen and the book is at the charming village church. It was here Jane set the marriage of Elinor Dashwood and Edward Ferrars. Visitors will have no difficulty recreating the joyful moment the happy couple come out of the church and through the lychgate. From here the walker must head towards Brampford Speke until they come to a bridleway on the edge of woodland. This leads to Woodrow Barton, a series of farm buildings which sit less than a mile from the church. This is believed to be the Barton Cottage of the novel. Pynes - the house where Jane Austen resided during her stay - is only half-a-mile from here. The 18th-century house also featured in the novel, becoming the home of Sir John and Lady Middleton.

Jane also fell in love with the delights of Dawlish during her stay in the area. The popular resort gets a mention in Sense and Sensibility, forming one of the many amusing moments in the book. Robert Ferrars presumes Elinor Dashwood lives at Dawlish when she tells him she resides at a cottage in Devon. When she puts him right, informing him she actually lives four miles north of Exeter, Ferrars is somewhat surprised, believing it impossible for anyone to live in Devon without living near Dawlish!

Another writer who resided on the outskirts of Exeter was novelist EDEN PHILLPOTTS. He spent the final few years of his life in the village of Broadclyst, which can be found six miles north-east of the city. He died at his Kerswell home in 1960 at the age of 98. The immediate area north of Exeter is sparsely populated and has therefore very few literary connections. One interesting place to visit is the village of Kentisbeare, near Cullompton. Here you will find some of the last lines novelist WALTER SCOTT ever wrote. Scott's cousin, the Rev George Scott, was rector of Kentisbeare Church from 1828 until 1830, when he died of scarlet fever at the age of 26. The epitaph Walter Scott wrote to his cousin can

The church at Upton Pyne was where Jane Austen set the marriage of Elinor Dashwood and Robert Ferrars.

be found in the church where the latter is buried.

Tiverton - a bustling town about 12 miles from Exeter - has a number of literary connections. Its famous Blundell's School was immortalised by R.D. BLACKMORE in Lorna Doone. Blackmore - who was himself a former pupil - places John Ridd at the school and opens the book within its grounds. Farmhand John Fry comes to collect John to take him home, all the time concealing the fact John's father has been murdered by Carver Doone. The two lodge at the White Horse Inn in Gold Street, opposite the Greenway Almshouses, before making the long journey home.

The school was founded by wealthy clothier Peter Blundell. Old Blundell's School was built in 1604 and converted to dwellings in 1880 when the school moved to its present location less than a mile away. The old building is now owned by the National Trust.

Tiverton was also the birthplace of the remarkable playwright HANNAH COWLEY. She never dreamed of writing until she went to the theatre and left disappointed one evening. She did not like the play in question and told friends she could produce something far more entertaining. Within two weeks, The Runaway, the first of her many successful London plays, appeared. She went on to write about a dozen more plays, including The Belle's Stratagem. Hannah was born at Tiverton in 1743, the daughter of bookseller Philip Parkhurst, whose mother was a cousin of poet John Gay. She died in her home town in 1809.

JOHN KEATS

Poet John Keats became the most-widely read and familiar of the English Romantic poets. He was hailed as the greatest writer of his generation and often compared to Shakespeare. His work included the famous odes, Ode to a Nightingale and Ode on a Grecian Urn. He also gained fame for the epic, Endymion, a poem written on the South Devon coast.

Places to see: Teignmouth: Keats' House.

Poet John Keats spent a brief but important time of his life in the popular seaside resort of Teignmouth. Like many visitors to this part of South Devon, he came for the mild climate and reputable sunshine, and like many, left disappointed! He recorded how appalling the weather was in his letters home to London, describing Devon as a 'splashy, rainy, misty, snowy, foggy, haily, floody, muddy, slipshod county'!

The town had a growing reputation as a health resort. Keats came in March 1818 to tend to his brother Tom who was dying from consumption. It was hoped the 'mild' climate would be of some benefit! When he first arrived Keats complained of not being able to get out.

'Being agog to see Devonshire, I would have taken a walk the first day, but the rain would not let me, and the second, but the rain would not let me; and the third....' I think we get the picture, John! It does not always rain in Teignmouth, however, so the poet's despairing words should not put you off retracing his steps.

A plaque on a cottage at narrow Northumberland Place informs visitors where he lodged. Keats' House, as it is now called, is not open to the public, but still one of the most-popular tourist attractions in the town. Because of the weather, Keats spent most of his three-month stay in the cottage. This gave him time to tend to Tom and produce some of his greatest work. Endymion was completed within these walls. He also wrote Isabella, or The Pot of Basil at 20 Northumberland Place. Apart from the cottage there is little physical evidence of the poet's stay.

Poet John Keats penned some of his finest work at 20 Northumberland Place, Teignmouth.

A nice walk from Teignmouth is across Shaldon Bridge and along the coast to Babbacombe, Torquay. Keats, in his letters, said only the rain had prevented him from completing the trek. He had intended walking all the way to Kent's Cavern. It is not known whether he did finally make it.

He also enjoyed the surrounding villages of Bishopsteignton and Combeinteignhead and spoke of them fondly in one of his many poems on the area. The neighbouring town of Dawlish is only three miles away. A nice walk is along the sea wall to Holcombe and then via the sporadic coast path. Keats made the journey to Dawlish himself when he visited Dawlish Fair.

John Keats only stayed for three months and was back in London by May. Sadly, the great Romantic poet caught the illness from Tom and was also dead within three years.

All the visitor needs to make their visit to Teignmouth and the home of Keats really authentic is the rain - maybe not!

Teignmouth was also home to poet and politician WINTHROP MACKWORTH PRAED. He spent most of his early childhood in the seaside town. The family seat was Bitton House overlooking the beautiful Teign Estuary. The grand building - now home of the town council - featured in Praed's work when he wrote under the name of Peregrine Courtenay. Teignmouth and the surrounding area is described fondly in much of his work.

Praed became co-editor of the famous English School journal, The Etonian, and later served as a Member of Parliament. His illness- stricken life ended in 1839. Praed was buried in London, but the family memorial can be found in the churchyard at St James' Church, Teignmouth.

Bitton House has another literary connection, courtesy of a former owner. Lord Exmouth - alias Sir Edward Pellew - was the inspiration for Captain Horatio Hornblower, the creation of C.S. FORESTER. Lord Exmouth - he was prevented from taking the title of the town as there was already a Baron Teignmouth - gained fame during the Siege of Algiers. Hornblower's adventures are based on incidents which occurred in Lord Exmouth's life.

FANNY BURNEY - the famous diarist and novelist - was also a regular visitor to Teignmouth. She stayed at the home of her sister, Martha Rishton, and took time to describe the town in great detail, commenting particularly on its hard-working women, who did everything from the housework to going out fishing!

JOHN DRYDEN

Poet and dramatist John Dryden was one of the most-important literary figures of the late 17th century. The versatile writer was a former Poet Laureate; wrote comedies and tragedies, and was regarded as the first great English critic. He was also known for his strong political and religious views. Dryden was a frequent visitor to the county, lodging at elegant Ugbrooke House.

Places to see: Ugbrooke House.

Ugbrooke House is situated close to Chudleigh, just off the busy A380 Newton Abbot to Exeter road. A grove of beech trees in the grounds of the house form what is now called Dryden's Walk. The poet stayed at Ugbrooke House when his friend Lord Clifford was the owner in the mid-1680s. He is believed to have written part of The Hind and the Panther while staying here. Visitors to the gardens can sit on Dryden's Seat - reputed to be the spot where he composed some of the lines of the fable. A visit to Ugbrooke House is well worth the effort, but the visitor should be aware it is privately-owned and has limited opening times.

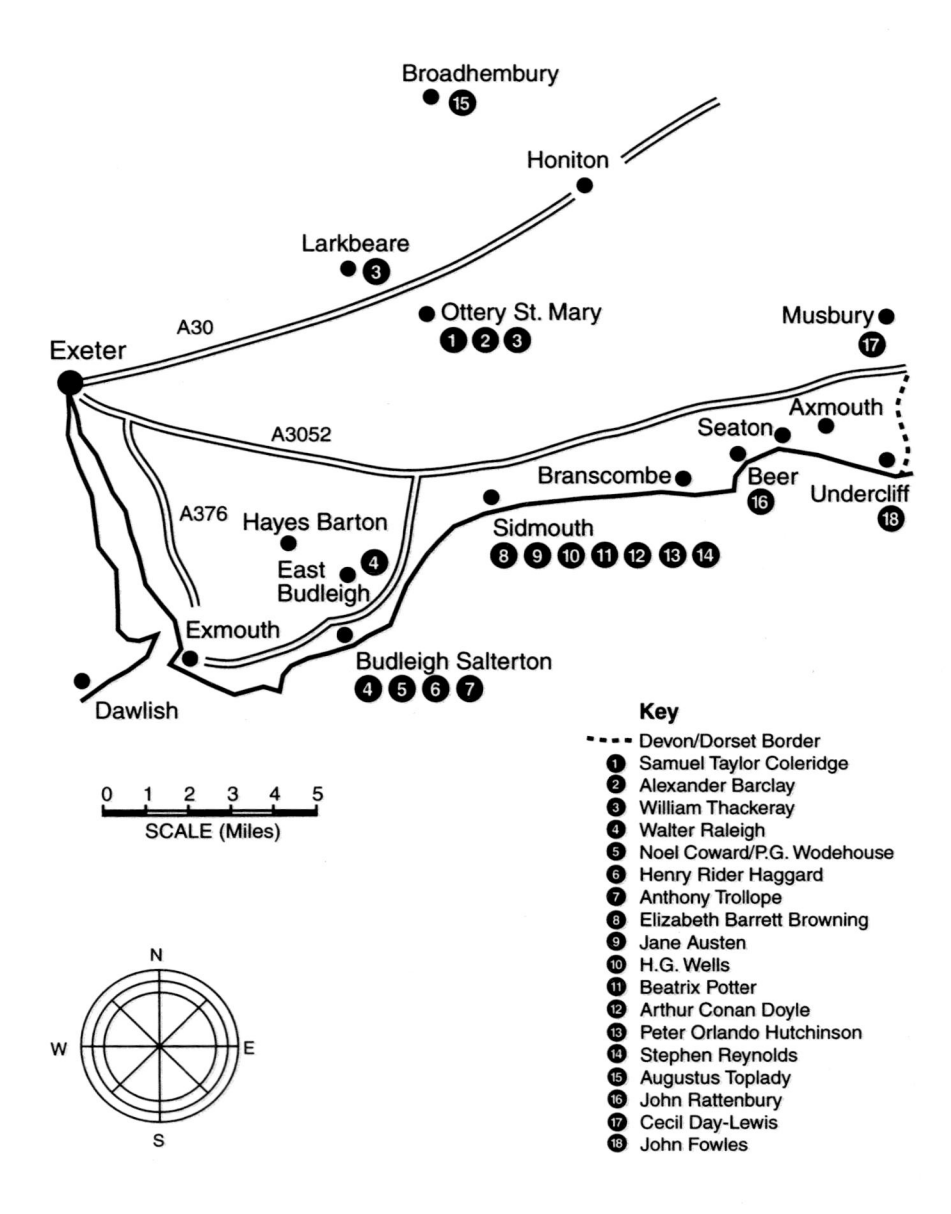

EAST DEVON

EAST DEVON

Broadhembury ● ⑮

Honiton ●

Larkbeare ● ❸

A30

Exeter ●

● Ottery St. Mary
❶❷❸

Musbury ● ⑰

A3052

Seaton ●

Axmouth ●

Branscombe ●

Beer ●
⑯

Undercliff ⑱

A376

Hayes Barton ●

Sidmouth
❽❾❿⓫⓬⓭⓮

● ❹
East Budleigh

Exmouth ●

Budleigh Salterton
❹❺❻❼

Dawlish ●

0 1 2 3 4 5
SCALE (Miles)

Key
- - - - Devon/Dorset Border
❶ Samuel Taylor Coleridge
❷ Alexander Barclay
❸ William Thackeray
❹ Walter Raleigh
❺ Noel Coward/P.G. Wodehouse
❻ Henry Rider Haggard
❼ Anthony Trollope
❽ Elizabeth Barrett Browning
❾ Jane Austen
❿ H.G. Wells
⓫ Beatrix Potter
⓬ Arthur Conan Doyle
⓭ Peter Orlando Hutchinson
⓮ Stephen Reynolds
⓯ Augustus Toplady
⓰ John Rattenbury
⓱ Cecil Day-Lewis
⓲ John Fowles

N / W / E / S

A combination of charming seaside resorts and glorious rolling countryside persuaded many writers to look for their inspiration in this part of the county. The popular Victorian resorts of Budleigh Salterton and Sidmouth attracted numerous distinguished literary greats. Many, such as Elizabeth Barrett Browning, came for the mild climate, while others sought the relaxed atmosphere which is still evident even today. It is, however, a home-grown talent - poet Samuel Taylor Coleridge -who can stake the biggest claim to putting East Devon on the literary map.

SAMUEL TAYLOR COLERIDGE
Samuel Taylor Coleridge was one of the country's leading Romantic poets. He is best-remembered for The Rime of the Ancient Mariner, which he wrote while living at Nether Stowey on the edge of the Quantock Hills in Somerset. His early years were spent in East Devon - an area which also had an influence on much of his work.

Places to see: Ottery St Mary: Ottery St Mary Church - Pixies' Parlour.

Ottery St Mary sits at the heart of East Devon. It is the perfect place to begin a literary tour of the area, being the birthplace of one of the country's most-popular poets. Samuel Taylor Coleridge was born at the vicarage of Ottery St Mary Church in 1772. He was the 13th and youngest child of the Rev John Coleridge - one of the leading figures in the town at the time. Coleridge senior - apart from being a vicar - was also headmaster of the King's Grammar School. The church which he served and where Samuel spent his early life still dominates the town and is well worth a visit. A plaque in honour of the poet can be found on the churchyard wall. It is not difficult to imagine the young Samuel playing among the gravestones. He spent many hours in the churchyard, which was situated opposite the old School House, where his father taught. It is believed his childhood was an unhappy one, even though he looked back upon it fondly in many of his poems. The bells of Ottery St Mary were described affectionately in Frost at Midnight, which was a romanticised version of his childhood. He describes his birthplace as 'sweet' but Coleridge was a dreamer and found it difficult to mix with other boys.
He was undoubtedly a clever child - by the age of three he was already attending the local dame school and could read whole chapters from the Bible. In 1779, he was allowed to attend King's School, but in his first year he was struck down by a fever and was dangerously ill in isolation at the top

of the School House. It was here young Samuel had his first nightmares, which were to haunt him for the rest of his life. Many of these visions were described in his poems.

One trek worth making - if you can find the destination - is to the young poet's secret hideaway. Pixies' Parlour was a sandstone cave situated in a field overlooking the River Otter a mile south of the town. Coleridge joined his peers in carving his initials on the cave walls and found them still there when he returned on a nostalgic visit many years later as an under-graduate. Songs of the Pixies, and numerous other poems, were inspired by the cave. The cave is situated on a wooded sandstone ridge, about 50 yards from the eastern bank of the river. An Ordnance Survey map will aid your search. The young Coleridge loved the countryside around him and was particularly fond of walking along the river. He penned a sonnet To the River Otter in appreciation. The visitor to Ottery St Mary can also stroll along the river's edge as there are riverside walks in both directions.

Coleridge was just nine when his beloved father died. The family were forced to move out of the vicarage and stay in temporary accommodation at the nearby Warden's House. He was eventually sent packing to Christ's Hospital in London, which was a charity school set up for sons of needy clergy. The youngster did not grieve for Ottery St Mary or his mother and revelled

Samuel Taylor Coleridge is immortalised on the churchyard wall at Ottery St. Mary Church.

in the capital. He only returned to his birthplace on nostalgic visits.

Ottery St Mary also became the home of poet-priest ALEXANDER BARCLAY in 1509. It was in the town, while serving as chaplain at the College of Ottery St Mary, he translated Sebastian Brant's satiric Narrenschiff into English as The Ship of Fools. The work contained some personal attacks on local Devon clergy. Barclay was one of the country's first pastoral poets.

WILLIAM MAKEPEACE THACKERAY

Novelist William Makepeace Thackeray is best-remembered for the classic Vanity Fair, which was published in serial form from 1847 to 1848. He spent many childhood holidays in East Devon - experiences which were later to influence his work.

Coleridge often played among the gravestones at his father's church.

Places to see: Ottery St Mary. Larkbeare.

Larkbeare is situated on the outskirts of Ottery St Mary. It was here the young Thackeray spent many school holidays with his stepfather. He got to know the area well and used it many years later when he was writing The History of Pendennis. Many places and people were loosely disguised under fictional names. Ottery St Mary became Clavering St Mary - the birthplace of

Arthur Pendennis, while the River Otter was renamed, the River Brawl. Neighbouring towns, which Thackeray frequently visited, also featured. Exeter became Chatteris and Sidmouth became Baymouth. Thackeray did his own illustrations for his novels. The first edition of Pendennis contained a vignette of the north tower of Ottery St Mary Church. The book, which followed the hugely-successful Vanity Fair, was published in serial form from 1848 to 1850.

Larkbeare is situated about two miles north-west of Ottery St Mary. It is not open to the public.

WALTER RALEIGH

The literary work of Walter Raleigh has not surprisingly been overshadowed by his own seafaring exploits. He penned tales of his many epic voyages throughout the world and also found time to write poetry. Raleigh's famous, The History of the World, was written during his imprisonment in the Tower and published unfinished in 1614. His literary work also included A Report of the Truth of the Fight about the Isles of Azores, which focused on another seafaring Devonian - Richard Grenville.

Places to see: Budleigh Salterton. East Budleigh: Hayes Barton.

The elegant resort of Budleigh Salterton is a fine place to begin a short tour of Walter Raleigh's home. The town has changed much from the days when the young Walter would have come here, but as most resorts go, it remains uncommercial and still has a certain charm to it.

Standing on the pebble beach you will not find it difficult to imagine the young boy looking out to sea, dreaming of foreign lands. Artist John Millais certainly had no problems and painted his classic Boyhood of Raleigh using the ancient wall which still stands on the beach.

The Fairlynch Museum at Fore Street has information on both Raleigh and Millais.

Raleigh was actually born at Hayes Barton on the outskirts of East Budleigh, which is situated about two miles north of Budleigh Salterton. East Budleigh is a charming village full of thatched cottages. It honours its most-famous son through the Sir Walter Raleigh Inn - a perfect place to rest your weary feet and take refreshment.

A road opposite - it is clearly sign-posted - will lead the visitor to Hayes Barton. The Tudor farmhouse is found about one mile along the lane. The privately-owned building is not open to the public, but it can be viewed from

Elegant Hayes Barton at East Budleigh was the birthplace of Walter Raleigh.

the roadside without any problem. It has become one of the most-photographed buildings in all of Devon.

Budleigh Salterton was once a fashionable resort and attracted many important figures. It also became a stock joke in London's theatres, being portrayed as a genteel resort where nothing much happened. NOEL COWARD and P.G. WODEHOUSE were among those who partook in the affectionate mocking through their work.

There is no doubting Budleigh Salterton is quieter than the average seaside resort - though many think that is its appeal! This was not the case for novelist HENRY RIDER HAGGARD, however. He stayed here during World War One to escape the bombs of London and to write what was to be his last major novel - When the World Shook.

But Haggard, best-known for the adventure King Solomon's Mines, found Budleigh Salterton too quiet - to the point of exasperation! He wrote home to say he could not stand it any longer; packed his bags and returned to the war-torn capital!

Another visitor - though he found it much more pleasant - was novelist ANTHONY TROLLOPE. He came on several occasions to visit his brother Thomas Adolphus Trollope, who lived at a corner house in Cliff Terrace at the junction with Cliff Road. Sadly, the building no longer exists. Thomas, himself a writer, was five years older than his more illustrious brother.

ELIZABETH BARRETT BROWNING

The charming resort of Sidmouth is found four miles further along the coast. Poet Elizabeth Barrett Browning was just one of those who came to reap the benefits of the area's mild climate. The town was to play an important part in her life.

Places to see: Sidmouth: Fortfield Terrace - Nortongarth - Cedar Shade.

Sidmouth became home to poet Elizabeth Barrett Browning in 1832. Plagued by ill-heath throughout her life, she came to the county in the hope its mild climate would improve her consumption. The family settled at a house in Fortfield Terrace, which was once occupied by the Grand Duchess Helena of Russia. A plaque on the wall of the current building records the fact. A replica of the Russian Eagle still stands on the roof of the building. The family stayed here for less than a year before moving across the road to a larger house known today as Nortongarth. The final few months of their three-year spell at Sidmouth were spent at Belle Vue in All Saints Road. It is now known as Cedar Shade.

Elizabeth worked on Prometheus Bound while living in the resort. It was here she also met the Rev George Hunter, the non-conformist minister of Marsh Chapel, who fell hopelessly in love with her. He tried in vain to win her heart and only gave up when he realised poet Robert Browning had won it some 13 years later. Under the Rev Hunter's influence, Elizabeth wrote a number of hymns and poems. She left Sidmouth for London in 1835 but returned to the county three years later, this time choosing to reside at Torquay.

Another who attracted eyes from a local member of the clergy was novelist JANE AUSTEN. During her stay at Upton Pyne, near Exeter, Jane visited Sidmouth and reputedly fell in love with a clergyman. Jane was a quiet and secret woman, so little is known about the meeting and the man's identity has remained a mystery. It is believed he proposed to her, though it is not known whether she accepted. Some say Jane received a letter shortly after their meeting to say he had died. Her grief is later poured out in Sense and Sensibility. The author set the honeymoon destination of Robert and Lucy at Sidmouth. The resort is also believed to have been the model for the unfinished novel Sanditon, even though the author gave it a Sussex location. Other writers inspired by Sidmouth include H.G. WELLS. The popular science-fiction writer set his short-story, The Sea Raiders, around Jacob's Ladder - a popular spot found at the western end of the beach.

Children's author BEATRIX POTTER was another inspired by the East

Devon countryside, though she was prompted to take up her brush rather than a pen! She is known to have visited Sidmouth in 1902 and painted a view of the beach and cliffs.

ARTHUR CONAN DOYLE - creator of Sherlock Holmes - was another visitor. He came to the resort to play cricket with the MCC. There are many who say Doyle conceived the idea for The Hound of the Baskervilles while he was actually playing. He was said to have been put off by the sound of howling dogs!

Sidmouth succeeded in attracting many distinguished visitors, but has also had some interesting residents itself. Historian and diarist PETER ORLANDO HUTCHINSON spent most of his life in the town. Much of it was spent collecting material for his five-volume History of Sidmouth. He began the mammoth task in 1849 and finally completed Volume Five in 1880 at the age of 70! Hutchinson came to Sidmouth as a teenager and stayed until his death, becoming one of the town's most-celebrated characters.

Novelist STEPHEN REYNOLDS also knew the importance of research. For his popular novel, A Poor Man's House, a story about the life of a Sidmouth fisherman and his family, Reynolds left behind middle-class society to live and work with the poor. Sidmouth appears as Seacombe in the book. Just a couple of miles north of the town is Harpford Wood and the Church of St Gregory. Hymn-writer AUGUSTUS TOPLADY - the author of Rock of Ages - served here for two years as vicar from 1766. He later moved to Broadhembury, near Honiton, where he served for a further ten years. A plaque can be found on the wall of the church chancel at the latter.

JOHN RATTENBURY

Smuggler John Rattenbury can hardly be described as a great writer - he was illiterate to start with - but he left behind one of the most-remarkable books ever to be written. Memoirs of a Smuggler was published in 1837. It contained his own personal insight into the West Country smuggling trade while it was at its height. The notorious Rattenbury achieved a celebrity-like status and was prevailed upon to relate his many adventures encountered during more than 30 years in the trade. He was born in the pretty coastal village of Beer.

Places to see: Beer - coast path between Branscombe and Seaton - Bovey House.

At first glance it is difficult to believe the charming fishing village of Beer was once the centre of Devon's smuggling industry. Explore the surrounding cliffs, however, and you will have no trouble imagining Rattenbury and his colleagues landing their booty on these shores. John Rattenbury was born at Beer in 1778. He lived most of his life in the village and enjoyed many scrapes with the authorities here.

Two charming cliff walks will reveal the many places described by Rattenbury in his memoirs. The one-mile cliff walk from Beer to Seaton begins at Jubilee Gardens. This is believed to be the spot where customs officer Robert Head was stationed. His house had a perfect view of the beach and any illegal activities going on directly out at sea. Head was in charge of a small team of preventative officers stationed at Beer. Their presence deterred the landing of goods on Beer Beach and forced smugglers to ply their trade in less obvious openings all along the coast. From Jubilee Gardens the walker soon reaches the heights of White Cliff. This was where smugglers lit fires to signal to colleagues out at sea to warn them if it was safe to come ashore. Seaton Hole - sitting midway between Beer and Seaton - was a convenient landing place for goods, being so close to a road. It became one of Rattenbury's most-popular haunts. Seaton Chan - a mere quarter of a mile from Seaton - was another landing spot, though less frequented. The small break in the cliffs also connected to a road to give the receivers the chance to make a quick exit.

In the other direction from Beer is Beer Head and Pound's Pool, a quarter of a mile below Beer. Here the goods were landed under the cliff and hauled up to the top by ropes. Another excellent landing spot was a mile away at Hooken. Many years ago ten acres of the cliff crumbled into the sea, forming a small cove. This became a secret place for large quantities of goods to be landed and carried up to the top of the cliff via a winding path. A similar operation took place at Mitchell's Stile, another half-mile along. Branscombe Mouth - a similar distance away - was another favourite spot because of a road leading up to Branscombe Village.

Bovey House - just over a mile inland from Beer - was once used as a rendezvous by smugglers during a period when the building was empty. The smugglers did their best to perpetuate the legend of the house being haunted by a lady in a blue silk dress!

Rattenbury not only describes his favourite haunts in his memoirs, but also boasts about his many escapes from customs officers. His most-famous escape took place at a pub in Beer - possibly the Dolphin, Anchor or New Inn. Rattenbury claims he was surrounded by a dozen armed militiamen with just a knife in his hand. The sergeant ordered his men to seize Rattenbury, but the terrified soldiers, such was the smuggler's fearful reputation, stood rigid and a four-hour stalemate ensued. Rattenbury finally made his escape during a lapse in concentration on the side of his aggressors.

Four miles north-east of Seaton Bay is the village of Musbury. Irish poet and novelist CECIL DAY-LEWIS moved here in 1938 and quickly fell in love with the surrounding countryside. The Buried Day contains many fond descriptions. His stay was interrupted by the Second World War when he was forced to move to London to take up a post with the Ministry of Information. Day-Lewis wrote detective novels under the name Nicholas Blake.

JOHN FOWLES

Novelist John Fowles is the author of The French Lieutenant's Woman, which was set on the Devon/Dorset border. The novel was largely written in pastiche Victorian prose and contained two separate endings.

Places to see: The Undercliff (coast path from Axmouth to Lyme Regis).

A fine literary walk is along the famous Undercliff which runs along the coast into the tip of both Devon and Dorset. The six-mile stretch of coast from Axmouth to Lyme Regis is known as The Landslip because of the catastrophe which occurred here. On Christmas Day 1839, part of Dowland Cliff collapsed into the sea taking trees and houses with it. The Undercliff which formed has remained virtually untouched by man and is now a haven for wildlife.

In The French Lieutenant's Woman, John Fowles describes The Undercliff as one of the strangest coastal landscapes in Southern England.

Though much of the action in the book takes place at Lyme Regis on the Dorset side, Fowles does take his characters across the border into Devon. Charles Smithson - the hero of the novel - searches the crumbling slopes of Pinhay Bay for fossils and meets beautiful Sarah Woodruff here. The Devon/Dorset border is marked by Ware. The walker should realise once they have begun their trek from Axmouth there is little opportunity of escape, so must retrace their steps or journey all the way to Lyme Regis.